A Book
Of Learned
·Nonsense·

The Spectacled Owlet
or the Learned nonsensical jargon Bird

'The Spectacled Owlet or Learned Nonsensical Jargon Bird' – a sketch by
Edward Lear's friend, Ward Braham, September 1872.

A BOOK
OF LEARNED
·NONSENSE·

A Centenary Anthology of
Writings & Sketches by

EDWARD LEAR

EDITED BY
PETER HAINING

W.H. ALLEN · LONDON
1987

Copyright © Peter Haining, 1987

Set in Bembo by Phoenix Photosetting, Chatham
Printed and bound in Great Britain by
Mackays of Chatham Ltd, Chatham, Kent
for the publishers, W.H. Allen & Co. Plc
44 Hill Street, London W1X 8LB

ISBN 0 491 03196 3

Design by Cecil Smith

For
My Daughter, Gemma

Some more Learical Lyrics
For your Loquacious Library!

CONTENTS

Saith the Poet of Nonsense:
'Thoughts into my head do come,
Thick as flies upon a plum.'
San Remo, 31 October 1881.

ONE

EDWARD LEAR: 'LORD HIGH BOSH AND NONSENSE PRODUCER'

AN INTRODUCTION

n the winter of 1862, Edward Lear informed one of his closest friends, Chichester Fortescue, that he was proposing to write to the Chancellor of the Exchequer, Mr Gladstone, 'and ask him to make me Grand Peripatetic Ass and Boshproducing Luminary'. A year later, he had apparently set his sights even higher and told the same correspondent he wanted the Prime Minister, Lord Palmerston, 'to ask the Queen to ask the King of Greece to give me a "place".' The 'place' he had in mind, he said, was as 'Lord High Bosh and Nonsense Producer' – and would Fortescue as a Member of Parliament use his best offices to secure this position!

One hundred years after Lear's death, there is no disputing

that he deserves both these titles and others of a more serious nature. But there were, in fact, no honours for this incredibly creative and complex man during his life – though he did, at least, live long enough to read himself described in *The Spectator* just four months before his death as 'the parent of modern nonsense writers'. The review, in the issue of 17 September 1887, added: 'He is distinguished from all his followers and imitators by the superior consistency with which he has adhered to his aim – that of amusing his readers by fantastic absurdities.'

These words still ring true today, though it is a surprise to learn that Lear's reputation went into something of a decline in the years immediately after his death on 29 January 1888. However, the twentieth century has seen the re-establishment of his fame and no modern generation has found itself able to resist the 'meloobious and fangropunxious feelings' engendered by reading his verses and lyrics.

It is for his Nonsense Books, of course, that Lear is best known, but he was also (apart from being a superb painter and draughtsman) an outstanding humorist and comic writer – as I hope the pages of this centenary anthology will show. For Lear poured his seemingly inexhaustable sense of fun into *everything* he wrote, whether it was the journals of his travels, his letters, or in scraps of poetry and prose written for the amusement of his friends and their children. It has been my task – and pleasure – to resurrect these 'Scribblebibbles', 'Puffles of Prose' and 'Learical Lyrics' (as he variously referred to them), not to mention his 'Landskipper Letters' and 'Journal Gleanings' to celebrate his contribution to the world of humour.

It has been rather like repaying an old debt. For my childhood, like that of millions of other youngsters, was enchanted by the exploits of the Owl and the Pussycat, amused by the Old Man of the Coast (who placidly sat on a post) – not forgetting all his other nonsensical associates – and puzzled by who or why or which or what was the Ahkond of Swat? Indeed, I have retained a delight in Edward Lear's small library of books into adulthood and in turn have introduced them into the bed-time reading of my own children.

But by far the most influential moment in the development of my admiration for Edward Lear occurred when I had my first sight of some of his original drawings. This happened while I was holiday in Somerset some years ago and had cause to visit the Somerset Records Office at Taunton. For here are lodged a number of his unique and unmistakable sketches, including a comical self-portrait standing on a bench while painting, a whimsical picture of himself riding on the back of a porpoise, another drawing of himself and his servant, Giorgio, riding on the back of an elephant, and, finally, a portrait of none other than the bizarre and cross-eyed Ahkond of Swat!

As I examined those four sketches, made between the years 1860 and 1875 and all drawn in sepia ink on small sheets of writing paper, they seemed to me to represent a kind of

summary of the artist's life and work. Indeed, they reminded me of something Lear had once written. 'Nonsense,' he said, 'is the breath of my nostrils.'

For there in the sketches I could see a fine painter who could mock himself and had not been accorded the recognition his talent deserved. (Several galleries refused to hang his pictures while he was alive and Christie's would not even auction his work.) There was a restless traveller who delighted in communicating his experiences with others yet ultimately found only personal loneliness. (He fought a life-long battle between his religious convictions and repressed homosexua-

lity.) And, perhaps most strikingly of all, there was a man of unbounded good humour whose ability to depict the absurd disguised his own cripped life. (He had poor eyesight and regularly suffered epileptic fits).

Yet, equally, also to be found in those same pictures was the essence of what had earned him his enduring fame. For as his first biographer Angus Davidson wrote in *Edward Lear: Landscape Painter and Nonsense Poet* (1938), 'It was in Lear's comic drawings, as in his nonsense poems, that he showed his greatest, his supreme, originality, for here he invented something that had never been done before . . . Lear, when he made these drawings, was playing with his own skill, quietly amusing himself, just as he amused the children who watched him and greeted each new drawing and rhyme with cries of delight.'

Despite the enormous popularity that the nonsense illustrations and limericks enjoy today, the fact remains that only pure chance caused them to be published. For like those other creators of children's classics, Lewis Carroll with his adventures of Alice, and Beatrix Potter with her tales of small animals, Lear created his 'nonsenses' essentially for the children of friends, and it was only on the urgings of these friends, we believe, that the author finally issued the first collection called *A Book of Nonsense* in February 1846. The work actually appeared as two volumes, containing a total of 70 limericks and was issued by Thomas McLean, a graphic arts publisher in London's Haymarket. The volumes sold for three shillings and sixpence each and Lear did not append his name to either book, merely signing himself 'Old Derrydown Derry' on the title page.

There have been many explanations offered for the success of Lear's nonsense. The simplicity of the drawings matched to

the readability of the verses. The ingenious characters and their extraordinary experiences. The comic brilliance of his ideas and his skill at tapping a deep well-spring of humour.

Angus Davidson, for example, has this to say: 'Lear's great gift is that he can transport his reader into his strange world and make him accept its values, and it is in the incongruity of taking such values seriously that much of the humour lies. Yet "pure" nonsense such as Lear's is more than a mere absence of sense: it has an absolute value of its own; it enriches life with a new kind of wisdom; it is a true child of the imaginaton, and its native realm is poetry.'

For my part, I believe the explanation to be even simpler. Edward Lear knew how to reach the child in all of us. As a man who remained something of a child himself all his life, he knew instinctively how to enter the mind of children and did so through nonsense. If we can put to one side our adult scepticism, our cynicism and our world-weariness whenever we read him, our pleasure and laughter will be all the greater.

The reader might like to imagine his own reactions to receiving the following letter which Lear wrote to his friend, Evelyn Baring, later Lord Cromer – bearing in mind that this is one grown man writing to another:

'Thrippy Pilliwinx' Lear addresses his friend, 'Inkly tinky pobblebockle ablesquabs? Flosky! Beebul trimble flosky! Okul scratch abibblebongibo, viddle squibble tog-a-tog, ferry moyassity amsky flamsky damsky crocklefether squiggs!'

And the letter is signed, 'Flinky wisty pomm – SLUSHYPIPP.'

This is surely the ultimate nonsense, where words – so often abused in everyday use – are reconstituted for the simple pleasure of just *saying* them. And I defy anyone to read that letter without laughing or at least smiling a little . . .

The success of the Nonsense books was, we know, even something of a surprise to Lear. 'It is queer,' he wrote to Chichester Fortescue just after *More Nonsense* had been published in 1872, 'and you would say so if you saw me, that I am the man as is making some three or four thousand people laugh in England all at one time . . .'

Lear might find it queerer still, one hundred years later, to

The Akkond of Swat

discover his works still available and his readership running not into thousands, but millions.

Here, then, is my tribute to Edward Lear. None of the material herein appeared in Lear's own collections of nonsense, and items such as his letters and the extracts from his journals have been unavailable for a great many years, while much of the remaining text has been collected from original manuscript sources. The illustrations, too, have been assembled from a variety of sources including books, manuscripts and letters in collections on both sides of the Atlantic. It has been most satisfying for me to once again make this Lear memorabilia available, and I look for no better reward than that the shade of the author-artist might look down on me from whichever humorous heaven he is dwelling in and observe, as he once did of his friend, Chichester Fortescue, aka Lord Carlingford:

> Of Carlingford all nature knows –
> He paid his debts – he blew his nose!

PETER HAINING
Boxford, Suffolk
1 June 1987.

T W O

OLD
LANDSKIPPER'S
LETTERS

'Here is one more scrawl from
your troublesome old Landskipper.'
Edward Lear to Chichester Fortescue,
27 January 1884.

lthough Lear spent much of his life far from
the shores of England, his closest friends
were to be found in his native land and to
them he sent an unending stream of letters for
almost half a century. Unhappily, many of
these letters have since been lost or
destroyed, but fortunately a whole series of idiosyncratic and
intimate missives to his best friend, the parliamentarian Chichester Fortescue, have survived and in this first section I have
picked fifty-five of what I believe to be the most representa-
tive, interesting and above all humorous letters spanning a
period of thirty years from 1856 to his death.

Chichester Fortescue (1823–1898) was a privileged young
man who, after being educated at Oxford, took the traditional
'grand tour' of Europe and while in Rome in 1845 met the

struggling painter Edward Lear. Fortescue, who was then just twenty-two, was immediately taken with the artist ten years his senior, and after several more meetings noted in his diary that Lear was 'a delightful companion, full of nonsense, puns, riddles, everything in the shape of *fun*, and brimming with intense appreciation of nature as well as history. I don't know when I have met anyone to whom I took so great a liking.' These feelings were reciprocated just as keenly by Lear, and so began a friendship which was to endure until the day of the artist's death. Though the men spent remarkably few days actually in each other's company, the intimacy of their letters reveals a deep and abiding friendship. Indeed, in one of his letters, Lear wrote that he hoped the two men would at last be together after death 'when you and I are cherubim and sit on a tree above the waters of Paradise'! (His sketch of their 're-union' is featured on these pages!)

However, while Lear wandered the Continent in search of inspiration for his brush, Fortescue carved himself a career in British politics, becoming first the MP for Louth in Ireland, later the Chief Secretary for Ireland, President of the Board of Trade and finally Lord Privy Seal. In 1871 he married Frances, Lady Waldegrave, and in 1874 took the title Lord Carlingford. To Lear, though, he was always '40SCUE' (occasionally 'F' or 'Mimmbr' – for Member of Parliament) and it was by this affectionate sobriquet that he was always addressed in the letters which reached him from all over Europe, the Mediterranean and as far afield as India, signed with equal humour by the 'Old Landskipper'! Fortescue's wife he always addressed most respectfully as 'my Lady'.

Lear wrote to Carlingford in January 1853 that 'the more I read travels, the more I want to move,' and his letters are full of this enthusiasm for new places along with his eye for detail and his seeming knack of finding himself in amusing situations. The letters are, in many ways, the forerunners of some of his famous verses and lyrics, for not only are they frequently written in the same nonsensical style, but some of the people and situations clearly inspired some of his later humorous work. In them, too, the reader will come across references to others among Lear's close friends like the Poet

Laureate, Alfred, Lord Tennyson, his patron, Lord Northbrook, and Frank Lushington, a lawyer who later became a
judge, and was appointed Lear's literary executor – a rather
unsuitable choice, as it turned out, for he was responsible for
destroying many of the artist's papers, believing them to be
either of no value or indiscreet! And one must not forget
Giorgio Kokali, Lear's faithful servant from 1856 until his
death in 1883, when his eldest son took over the care of the
artist.

Lear wrote in a letter of July 1873 to '40SCUE' that 'There is
nothing like a Diary of letters for showing the real nature of a
writer.' Whether he had himself in mind when he penned this
one cannot be sure, but I believe the following edited selection
from his remarkable correspondence certainly takes us a little
closer to understanding the mind of the lonely genius who
created nonsense. The selection begins with a biographical
note which Lear wrote to his friend in 1862 outlining his life
and career: it provides an ideal preamble to the letters which
follow.

My Dear F. – I want to send you, before leaving England, a note or two as to the various publications I have uttered – bad and good, and of all sorts – also their dates, that so you might be able to screw them into a beautiful memoir of me in case I leave my bones at Palmyra or elsewhere. Leastwise, if a man does anything all through life with a deal of bother, and likewise of some benefit to others, the details of such bother and benefit may as well be known accurately as the contrary.

Born in 1812 (12th May), I began to draw, for bread and cheese, about 1827, but only did uncommon queer shop-sketches – selling them for prices varying from ninepence to four shillings: colouring prints, screens, fans; awhile making morbid disease drawings, for hospitals and certain doctors of physics. In 1831, through Mrs Wentworth, I became employed at the Zoological Society, and, in 1832, published *The Family of the Psittacidæ*, the first complete volume of coloured drawings of birds on so large a scale published in England, as far as I know – unless Audubon's were previously engraved. J. Gould's *Indian Pheasants* were commenced at the same time, and after a little while he employed me to draw many of his birds of Europe, while I assisted Mrs Gould in all her drawings of foregrounds, as may be seen in a moment by any one who will glance at my drawings in G.'s European birds and the Toucans. From 1832 to 1836, when my health failed a good deal, I drew much at the Earl of Derby's; and a series of my drawings was published by Dr Gray of the British Museum – a book now rare. I also lithographed many various detached subjects, and a large series of Testudinata for Mr (now Professor) Bell; and I made drawings for Bell's *British Mammalia*, and for two or more volumes of the *Naturalist's Library* for the editor, Sir W. Jardine, those volumes being the Parrots, and, I think, the Monkeys, and some Cats. In 1835 or '36, being in Ireland and the Lakes, I leaned more and more to landscape, and when in 1837 it was found that my health was more affected by the climate month by month, I went abroad, wintering in Rome till 1841, when I came to England and published a volume of lithographs called *Rome and its Environs*, Returning to Rome, I visited Sicily and much of the South of Italy, and continued to make chalk drawings, though in 1840 I had painted my two first oil-paintings. I also gave lessons in drawing at Rome, and was able to make a very comfortable living. In 1845 I came again to England, and in 1846 gave Queen Victoria some lessons, through Her Majesty's having seen a work I published in that year on the Abruzzi, and another on the Roman States. In 1847 I went through all Southern Calabria, and again went round Sicily, and in 1848

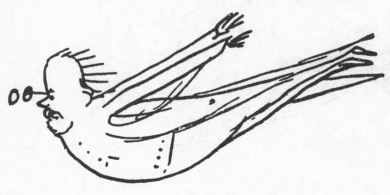

left Rome entirely. I travelled then to Malta, Greece, Constantinople, and the Ionian Islands; and to Mount Sinai and Greece a second time in 1849, returning to England in that year. All 1850 I gave up to improving myself in figure drawing, and I continued to paint oil-paintings till 1853, having published in the meantime, in 1849 and 1852, two volumes entitled *Journals of a Landscape Painter*, in Albania and Calabria. The first edition of the *Book of Nonsense* was published in 1846, lithographed by tracing-paper. In 1854 I went to Egypt and Switzerland, and in 1855 to Corfu, where I remained the winters of 1856–57–58, visiting Athos, and, later, Jerusalem and Syria. In the autumn of 1858 I returned to England, and '59 and '60 winters were passed in Rome. 1861, I remained all the winter in England, and painted the Cedars of Lebanon and Masada, going, after my sister's death in March, 1861, to Italy. The two following winters – '62 and '63 – were passed at Corfu, and in the end of the latter year I published *Views in the Ionian Islands*. In 1862 a second edition of the *Book of Nonsense*, much enlarged, was published, and is now in its sixteenth thousand.

O bother!

Yours affectionately,

EDWARD LEAR.

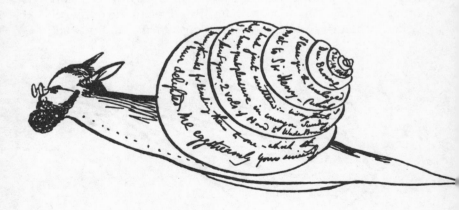

AMONG THE
MARMALADE MASTICATING MONX

Quarantine Island, Corfu, 9 October 1856.

PRIVATE and ΚΟΝΦΙΔΕΝΤΙΑL

I have just returned from a two month's tour, whereby I have seen and drawn all Mount Athos, and have seen Troy slightly. And whereby – which is far better – I have gained a great amount of health bodily and mentle, to my great satisfaction and I hope thankfulness, and also I trust to the benefit obliquely of many of my felly creatures who will hereafter peeroase my jurnles and admyer my pigchers.

I hope to paint a magnificent large view of Corfu straits and Albanian hills. This I trust to sell for £500 as it will be my best and is nine feet long. If I can't sell it, I shall instantly begin a picture 10 feet long; and if that don't sell, one 12 feet long. Nothing like persisting in virtue!

I got unwell and bluedevilled during the tour, and I made up my mind that I could work no more till something called out my boddly and mentle N.R.G.'s. So I said, I'll go to Mt. Athos. And off I set on August 7 taking my servant, Giorgio, canteen, bed and lots of paper and Quinine Pills.

There, getting better, I went slick into the Holy Mountain, altogether the most surprising thing I have seen in my travels. It is a peninsular mountain about 2,000 feet high and 50 miles long ending in a vast crag, near 7,000 feet high, this being Athos. All but this bare crag is one mass of vast forest, beech, chestnut, oak and ilex, and all round the cliffs and crags by the sea are 20 great and ancient monistirries, not to speak of 6 or 700 little 'uns above and below and around.

These convents are inhabited by, altogether perhaps, 6 or 7,000 monx, and as you may have heard, no female creature exists in all the peninsula – there is nothing but mules, tomcats and cocks allowed. This is literally true!

I got drawings of every one of the 20 big monasteries so that such a valuable collection is hardly to be found. Add to this constant walking – eight or ten hours a day – made me very strong, and the necessity I was under of acting decidedly in some cases, called out a lot of energy I had forgotten ever to have possessed.

The worst was the food and the filth which were uneasy to bear. However wondrous and picturesque the exterior and interior of the monasteries, and however abundantly and exquisitely glorious and stupendous the scenery of the mountain, I would not go again for any money, so gloomy, so shockingly unnatural, so lonely, so lying, so unatonably odious seems to me all the atmosphere of such monkery.

That half of our species which is natural to every man to cherish and love best, are ignored, prohibited and abhorred – all life spent in everlasting repetition of monotonous prayers, no sympathy with one's fellow beans of any nation, class or age. God's world and will turned upside down, maimed and caricatured – if this I say be Xtianity let Xtianity be rooted out as soon as possible.

More pleasing in the sight of the Almighty I really believe – and more like what Jesus Christ intended man to become – is an honest Turk with six wives or a Jew working hard to feed his little old clo' babbies, than these muttering, miserable, mutton-hating, man-avoiding, misogynic, morose and merriment-marring, monotoning, many-mule-making, mocking, mournful, minced-fish and marmalade masticating Monx. Poor old pigs!

So having seen all, and a queer page in my world-nollidge is Athos! – I came back to Salonika, and set sail for the Dardanelles, where being obliged to stay four days for a steamer, I spent three in seeing Troy. Thence I came by Sea to Corfu and be d---d to the owls for their folly!

A PEEK IN THE ARTIST'S STEWJEW

Corfu, 11 January 1857.

I must give you a short and serious account of myself. On coming out of Quarantine, a brutal Earthquake spifflicated my rooms and I had to remove and I thought it better to get an expensive place at once, on condition I could find a room for work. Whereby I took the ground floor of Scarpa's House on the Condi Terrace, or more properly speaking Bastione, St. Atanasio – for which I pay £6 a month.

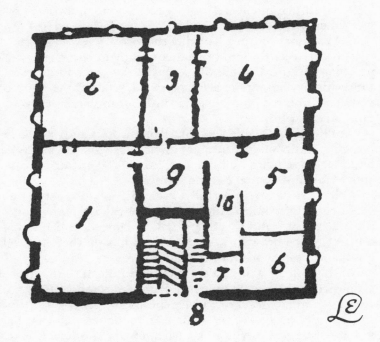

This is the plan of the baste.

1. Is my stewjew 30 feet long – windys all a looking to the North East, whereby the light is always perfect. This room I use only as a study – for learning Greek and

painting. My great nine feet canvas makes a good show of
work in it just now.

2. Is the sitting and dining room – very nice and
comfortable, library, good table, matting and very old
prints of Oxford Terrace around; Tennyson, Lord Derby
and Mr Hornby portraits; various Athos oddities here and
there.

3. Is a small and sinopothomostic chamber adorned with
my framed sketches and pick pictures as are finished for
people to come and see. Vich the coming of a live Markis
and Marchioness (Drogheda) and several other membiers of
the Peeriage vos the proudest moment of my life.

4. Is my bedroom plain and comfortable.

5. A lumber and spare room – to be done up proper for
you when you come visiting.

6. My man, Giorgio Kokali's room.

It is Mr Kokali's opinion and compliment that the
painting I am now doing of Corfu will prevent all other
Englishmen coming here, for he says, 'Where's the good of
people paying for coming so far if they can see the very
same thing at home?'

Giorgio is a valuable servant, capital cook, and endlessly
obliging and handy. Not quite as clean as I should always
like, but improving by kindness. I teach the critter to read
and write, and he makes long strides!

Well, I set to work fearfully, riz at 5½ always – at 6½ and
8½ the master comes. And then I paint till 3 or 4, having
breakfasted at 9 and I walk a bit till 6. Dine at 6½, and pen
out my Athos drawings till 10. My 'elth is on the 'ole pretty
good and I can work longer than before this year.

My big Corfu will be a stunner, and I mean to try for 500
guineas for him, he be nine feet four inches long, and six
feet 'i. I hope to get him to Manchester in time.

Here, my boy, give me your eternal thanks for what I am
going to suggest to you as a parliamentary motion. It is to
be brought out and spoken on by yourself, to the ultimate
benefit of society and to your own post-perpetual
glorification!

As soon as Parliament meets, move that all the distressed

needlewomen be sent out at once to Mount Athos! By this
dodge all the 5,000 monks young and old will be
vanquished! Distressed needle-babies will ultimately awake
the echoes of ancient Acte, and the whole fabric of
monkery, not to say of the Greek church, will fall down
crash and for ever!

N.B. Let the needlewomen be landed on the South-east
side of the peninsula and make a rush for the nearest
monastery, that subdued, all the rest will speedily follow!

THE WOMAN WHO
LOOKED LIKE A WHALE!

Royal Hospital, Dublin, 3 October 1857.

I shall write you a line, though there ain't much to say. I
travelled to Dublin safely, only discomposed a little because
the only person in the Railway compartment I got into was
a very fat woman, just exactly like a picture of Jonah's
whale I used to see when a child in a picture Bible.

I was horribly afraid she would eat me up and sat
expecting an attack constantly, till the arrival of the train
relived me of apprehension! At the Bilton I found a note
from that kind good Lady Seaton, saying that as an old
acquaintance of mine, Mr. Drummond and others had left
suddingly ther vos beds to spear. So went on and passed a
very pleasant evening.

I have pretty well made up my mucilaginous mind to
cross to Liverpool tonight. The day is highly beastly and
squondangerlous, and there is no fun going about in the
pouring rain in a car to make calls.

So, I shall very probably be in the Great Exhibition on
Tuesday after all. Stand in the second arch-place and
looking through the door you will see Syracuse. Goodbye,
my dear Mimmbr.

SEMISHUNTING TO PARIS

Pairlim Hotel, Folkestone, 20 November 1857.

All the ill luck and bad omens possible seemed to conspire to prevent my starting back for Corfu. First, the ticket master at Lewes gave me the wrong ticket (on my way to Bournemouth), so I hauled up at Brighton and nearly missed the Portsmouth train. But I didn't. Secondly, we ran into a semishunted goods train at Botlet and squashed our carriages! Happily, we were not going fast.

Meanwhile, my back was very badly jarred and I was unable to walk without great pain. Laying up next day at good Mrs. Empson's bettered me, and though still very lame, I am not getting over the wrench. At first, I thought I could not have started at all . . .

Today, at noon, I am going to start by the stereopyptic sophisticle steamer, and so on to Paris – the weather being miscelaynious and calm, thanks be to Moses!

Of *you*, I heard a grumpy man say a few days back, to my great pleasure, 'That Fortescue used to be the veriest idler and would have turned out good for nothing in spite of his head if he hadn't begun to work – but now he does, I can see, besides being told so!'

TALK OF TYMPANUM-TORTURING TURKEYS

Corfu, 9 January 1858.

O mi i! How cold it is!

The weather hasn't changed after all, and I believe don't mean to. It's as bright and cold and icicular as possible, and elicits the ordibble murmers of the cantankerous Corcyreans.

As for the English, they like the cold generally – I don't! Notwithstanding which, I must own to being in absolously better health than for I don't know how long past. Yesterday, I went up a mounting and made a sketch.

A majestic abundance of tympanum-torturing Turkeys are now met with on all the roads, coming into Corfu to be eaten. These birds are of a highly irascible disposition, and I never knew before two days ago that they objected to be whistled at!

But Colonel Campbell informed of the fact, and proved it to me, since when it is one of my peculiar happinesses to whistle at all the Turkeys I meet and see – and they get into such a damnable rage I can hardly stand for laughing!

After all, suppose a swell party in London – say at Cambridge House – if any one person began to whistle furiously at all the rest, wouldn't *they* get into a rage I should like to know?

I must leave off, I feel like five nutmeg-graters full of baked eggshells – so dry and cold and miserable!

THE ART OF PISTOL SHOOTING

Corfu, 9 March 1858.

O! here is a bit of queerness in my life. Brought up by women – and badly besides – and ill always, I never had any chance of manly improvements and exercise. I never touched firearms in all my days.

But you can't do work at the Dead Sea where I am going without them! So my friend Frank Lushington, who is always vy kind and good, makes me take a 5-barelled revoler and I have been practising shooting at a mark.

But I can hardly write for laughing at the thought of it! I have also learned all the occult nature of pistols. Don't grin.

My progress is slow – but always (I trust) somewhat!
At 103 I may marry possibly. Goodbye dear 40SCUE.
P.s. I've left you all my volumes of Leeke's *Greece* in case
of my being devoured by Arabs or fever.

THE HUSTLE-STREETS OF THE HOLY
CITY

Jerusalem, 1 April 1858.

During my stay here, this being the fifth day, every
moment has been occupied, or rather fussed away. Viz:
writing a long letter to my sister and a short line to
Lushington; walking all about the neighbouring hills to
understand its most pictural points; endless interviews with
interminable Dragomen, besides the hourly distraction of a
public Hotel chok full of people and the overcrowded state

of the streets. All this will give you some idea of the
landscape painter's state of body and mind . . .

The Holy City itself is just now in a most odious state of
suffocation and crowding, this one week uniting all sorts of
creeds and people in a disagreeable hodge-podge of curiosity
and piety. Lucky it was for me to get even the last single
room and one for my servant, and that day I was content to
give up struggling through the fearfully thronged hustle-
streets. And after a tabledhôte dinner was glad to be
thankful and sleep at Jerusalem, which I had so long wished
to see.

On Sunday the 28th, service in our church was a real
pleasure – well arranged, simple and good in all respects.
Afterwards my delight in going – on Palm Sunday, too – to
the Mount of Olives you can imagine. But the immense
beauty of the environs of Jerusalem you can*not* imagine, nor
could I before I saw it.

Meanwhile, I am off now to Bethlehem and Hebron in a
few hours: too glad to get some quiet from this noisy place!
Thence I go by the Dead Sea to Sebbeh (Masada), Engedi,
Mar Saba and Jericho and possibly beyond the Jordan.

THE SPLITMECRACKLE SINGER

9, Via Condotti, Rome, 24 January 1859.

I seem to have a great deal to say, but am scattery and shan't
write connectedly. I am not rejoiceful in Rome and cannot
'set myself in any good way'. I have no one with whom to
sympathize at all closely.

I wish indeed you were here for a time, but I trust to see
you in Ireland or England before next winter. The mass of
people here pass their lives in mere pleasure, a regular Bath
and Brighton life – and I don't care to know them. Others
are naturally using every moment in seeing sights and
learning Rome. Others have jealousies and smallness and

professional quirks from which I wholly stand aloof. O,
Lord, I wishes I was a beadle!

All the English fribble-world is irate about a Miss
Cavendish, whom Mrs. Hare a pervert has cajoled and
bebaptismalized, unbeknown to her parents. Cardinal
Manning is preaching the most atrocious sermons here, to
which nevertheless, all heaps of fools go.

A vile, beastly, rottenheaded, foolbegotten,
brazenthroated, pernicious, piggish, screaming, tearing,
roaring, perplexing, splitmecrackle, crashmecriggle, insane
ass of a woman is practising howling below-stairs with a
brute of a singingmaster so horribly, that my head is nearly
off!

OF COUGHS AND SNEEZES

15 Stratford Place, London, 4 November 1859.

O! Mimber for the County Louth
    Residing at Ardee!
Whom I, before I wander South
    Partik'lar wish to see: –

I send you this. – That you may know
    I've left the Sussex shore,
And coming here two days ago
    Do cough for evermore.

Or gasping hard for breath do sit
    Upon a brutal chair,
For to lie down in Asthma fit
    Is what I cannot bear.

Or sometimes sneeze: and always blow
    My well-develloped nose.
And altogether never know
    No comfort nor repose.

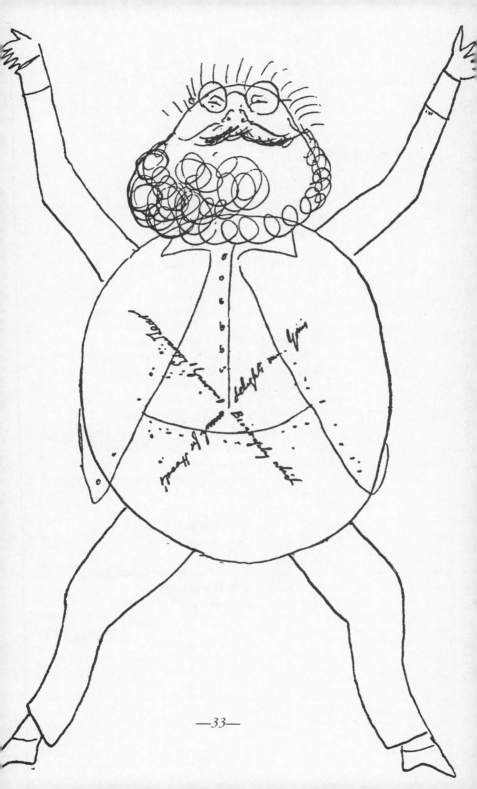

All through next week I shall be here,
    To work as best I may,
On my last picture, which is near-
    -er finished every day.

But after the thirteenth – (that's Sunday)
    I must – if able – start
(Or on the Tuesday if not Monday,)
    For England's Northern part.

And thence I only come again
    Just to pack up and run
Somewhere where life may less be pain,
    And somewhere where there's sun.

So then I hope to hear your ways
    Are bent on English moves
For that I trust once more to gaze
    Upon the friend I loves.

(Alas! Blue Posts I shall not dare
    To visit ere I go –
Being compulsed to take such care
    Of all the winds as blow.)

But if you are not coming now
    Just write a line to say so –
And I shall still consider how
    Ajoskyboskybayso.

No more my pen: no more my ink:
    No more my rhyme is clear.
So I shall leave off here I think –
    Yours ever,

                                    EDWARD LEAR.

ALL ROME IN A FRENZY

9 Via Condotti, Rome, 22 March 1860.

I am rather beshamed that I have not written to you for so long. And you are a cheerful cherub to send me the nice letter, dated the 13th, which has just been brought in by George, who says also, 'The revolution has been worked', alluding to what happened the night before last, of which anon. You in truth go on with wonderful 'Abercombiness' and regularity and the day will come when you will be as 43 giants.

Have you heard the story of the Echo of Villafranca? Here it is.

After their peace, the two Emperors, riding together, came to a place among the hills where there is a famous echo. France said, 'Que chacun de nouse appelle sa femma' to try the echo. So they did.

France called, 'Eugénie!' The echo answered, 'Génie!'

Austria called, 'Elizabèth!' The echo answered, 'Bête!'

We are all here in very disagreeable excitement – and on Monday night that occurred which is not yet wound up. It was Garibaldi's birthday and a festa besides – so that a considerable crowd walked in the Corso: for this kind of demonstration is the thing nowadays.

The police (armed) late in the day arrested two men who displayed nosegays of three colours but (this was in the Piazza Colonna) some French officers interfered and the two men were let loose. On which the Papal police retired 'green with rage'.

The Corso was full of people, just at Avemaria, when the police sallied out furiously, in all about 60, and ran amuck the whole length of the street to the Plaza del Popolo, cutting down and beating with buttend of pistols right and left.

You will hear all this denied by Lords Derby and Normanby, but as I know those who know the names of 35 seriously wounded now in Doctors' hands, and as the poor fruiter opposite my friend's died of his sword wound yesterday, and it is well known that altogether 70 or 80 were more or less hurt, you will excuse my believing the aristocratic defenders of Italy as it is, rather than my own senses.

As for me, I am at work on a heap of pictures, 20 in all: two of the Campagna, a Beyrout, Damascus and Interlaken. All will be striking topograffic scenes and I hope to sell them on my return to wise and wealthy wirtuous wights – for £700 if possible.

If things get more ojous here, I must leave earlier. A jew, a jew, my friend, I have become so fat for want of exercise that you would not know me, so I attach a portrait.

Do you wear knickerbockers? Don't you like Tithonus? Have you seen F. Lushington? Do you go to the Blue Posts? I must leave off like a deleterious donkey as I am –

Yours affly,
EDWARD LEAR

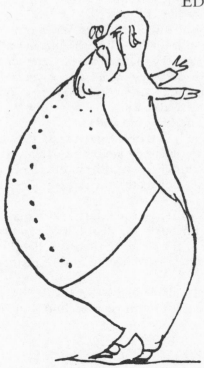

'A NASTY, UGLY OLD SCOTCHMAN!'

Oatlands Park Hotel, Surrey, 30 September 1860.

I will describe my life here generally. The Hotel is a large and sumptiously commodious place with nice broad terrace walks and a wonderfully lovely view over the river Temms and the surrounding landskip.

Them as likes private rooms, can have them. But, I and some 20 more live in public. I have a large, light bedroom, delightful to behold, and wanting for nought.

Here I rise to begin the day at 6, and by 6.30 or 6.45, am at work on one of the seven drawings. At 8 I go downstairs and from that to 9, breakfast audibly in the public coughy-room which is first-rate in every particular.

Immediately after these facts, I go out to work and by 6 I am back again. Dinner happens at 6.45 and is well arranged and good; and what pleases me I can get plain food. One pint of sherry and one ditto beer is my liquor.

The company is not bad and rather amusing: some is permanent, some changeful. Among the latter I trust are the parents of a beastly little child, whom seeing playing about, I spoke to simply as being attracted to all nice-looking children. Whereupon the imp thus accosted me:

'Oh, my! what an *ugly* chap you are! And what *ugly* shoes you wear! You must be a nasty, *ugly* old Scotchman!'

It is unnecessary to relate that I turned away with ill disguised disgust from this offensive infant, who cannot fail to bring his father's gray hairs to an untimely hend!

The only other person who has gone is a large old lady who the first night I was here, came slowly across the large reading room, steadily looking at me. When she had advanced within three feet of my chair, I could bear it no longer, for I knew she would do one of two things: either embrace me or charge me with a religious tract.

So I rose up in terror. At which she said in a loud voice,

'Sit down, Sir! I only came across the room to see if you was anyone I *knew*!'

The head waiter is a praiseworthy individual, and his efforts to make a goose go round 18 diners were remarkable yesterday – as well as his placid firmness when there was only one bit left and four persons yet unserved.

'Who's this for?' said an agitated buttony boy – foreseeing the invidiousness of the task set him.

'HENNYBODDY!' said the waiter in a decided tone. Then coming to the three gooseless persons, of whom I was one, he said in a conscientous and pained under-voice:

'Gentlemen, I am really sorry this has happened. But I declare to you that there shall be another goose *tomorrow*!'

At 9 I go to my room, much to the disgust of the community who, having found out that I am musical, consider my 'seclusion' unpleasant. And so they sent up a deputation two nights ago to ask me to come down to them – but I remained where I was.

For one hour I translate some Plato, and for one more hour I pen out some remaining Athos drawings. And at 11 I go to bed.

There's a pretty good history of life at the Oatlands Park Hotel!

All Greek To Me!

Corfu, 17 December 1861.

The present ephusion of my pen will be written in good sperrits because I have got to work and am working hard. Moreover, I got a letter from the printer of the *Book of Nonsense* who tells me that Routledge & Warne have brought it out and that over 500 copies been already sold! Please do what you can to encrease the sail by axing and talking about it.

What my letters are to you I can't say, for I never read

them over, but I believe they would be quite as fit to read 100 years hence as anybody elses naughty biography, specially when written off hand like mine are.

I wish I had more time for Greek: if I had my way and wor an axiom and Lawgiver, I would cause it to be understood that Greek is (or knowledge of it) the first of virtues. Cleanliness the second and Godliness – as held up by parsons generally – the third.

O mi hi! – here is a noo table, sicks feet too by three feet hate! I shall dine at one end of it – write at the other – and 'pen out' in the middle!

Do not cease adjuring people, especially Lord Shafestbury and the Bishop of Oxford, to buy the *Book of Nonsense*!

AN ANGELIC PLACE

Palaeokastrizza, Corfu, 20 April 1862.

I have been wondering if on the whole the being influenced to an extreme by everything in natural or physical life, i.e. atmosphere, light, shadow, and all the varieties of day and night – is a blessing or the contrary – and the end of my speculations has been that 'things must be as they may', and the best is to make the best of what happens.

I should, however, have added 'quiet and repose' to my list of influences, for at this beautiful place there is just now perfect quiet, excepting only a dim hum of myriad ripples 500 feet below me, all round the giant rocks which rise perpendicularly from the sea – which sea, perfectly calm and blue, stretches right out westward unbrokenly to the sky, cloudless save a streak of lilac cloud on the horizon.

On my left is the convent of Paleokastrizza, and happily, as the monkery had functions at 2 a.m. they are all fast asleep now. Also on the left is one of the many peacock-tail-hued bays here, reflecting the vast red cliffs and their crowning roofs of Lentish Prinari, myrtle and sage. Far above them, higher and higher, the immense rock of St. Angelo rising into the air, on whose summit the old castle still is seen a ruin, just 1,400 feet above the water.

It half seems to me that such life as this must be wholly another from the drumbeating bothery frivolity of the town of Corfu and I seem to grow a year younger every hour. Not that it will last. Accursed picnic parties with miserable scores of asses male and female are coming tomorrow, and peace flies – as I shall, too . . .

I hope this summer we may get a quiet two or three days together, for I take it after a short time you, the last of the Mohicans, will cease also to be single, at least I hope so, though the fact of your doubling yourself would cut you off more from my intercourse . . .

One thing, under all circumstances, I have quite decided on – when I go to heaven and am surrounded by thousands of polite angels, I shall say courteously:

'Please leave me alone! You are doubtless all delightful,

but I do not wish to become acquainted with you. Let me have a park and a beautiful view of sea and hill, mountain and river, valley and plain, with no end of tropical foliage.

'A few well behaved small cherubs to cook and keep the place clean, and, after I am quite established – say for a million or two of years – an angel of a wife.

'Above all, let there be no hens. No, not one! I gave up eggs and roast chicken for ever!'

Which rhapsody arises from a cursed infernal hen after having just laid an egg under my window and she screeches – O Lord! how she screetches – and will screech for an hour!

Wherefore, Goodbye. No more, dear friend, for at a screech I stop!

ALL AT SEA IN MALTA

Imperial Hotel, Valetta, 29 May 1862.

Here I am – still on my way Englandwards. But how it comes that I turned out of the Liverpool steamer, *Marathon*, and have been here since Sunday – I will now defulge.

I went on board the *Marathon* on Tuesday the 20th, believing she would start *directly* – and go *directly* to Liverpool. But she didn't start till Wednesday, and then, arriving at Zante she staid two whole days there: and so, by degrees, I heard it said that she would be ditto here, and at Messina and at Palermo and *might* reach England on the 10th or 12th of June. Witch faxs I only came at granulously as it were – grain by grain, as the pigeon said when he picked up the bushel of corn slowly.

Whereon – said I to myself – if so be as I can get my fare back again, I will even go ashore at Malta and see that much beloved place and wait for the Marseilles boat – thereby hoping to reach England before the 8th: and at a more convenient end, to wit, Newhaven or Dover. Meanwhile, resting my weary lims on beds of hashpodil, and moreover escaping the chance of bad weather in the Bay of Biscuits and the Irish Channel.

And to the honour and glory and pleasure of the *Marathon* be it said they guv me back my fare cheerfully – and have since gone on their way with the great lieutenant whom thou hast made to take his pastime therein.

The ship was a good ship: amzingly comfortable and thoroughly well conducted. Active and intelligent stewards pervaded the scene and enormous and globular stewardesses permeated behind the scenes. The food was good and plentiful, the ossifers friendly and pleasant.

But if the ship encountered a sea – O! wouldn't she roll! – being in form like a caterpillar, or right line – length without breadth. The company was select and rather quaint. Besides the Landscapepainter was the Lady of Sir Demetrius Valsamachi – once the wife of Bishop Heber – poor old lady! She was really very amiable and pleasant when awake or well enough to talk!

During the voyage I asked a fat Scotch stewardess, 'As you frequently stay here all about these ports, do you get fever?'

'O, Sir,' said she, with the strongest accent, 'I have fevers daily and nightly: the Lord God Almighty sends me fevers, even when I don't pray for them, and I am proud to think few is so highly fevered.'

By which I found she mistook fevers for favours!

She also suddenly went on (referring to Lady Valsamachi), 'Sir, is yon leddy the widdy of Bishop Heber or his daughter?'

'She is his widow,' said I.

'His widdy! And is it true then that she, a Christian Leddy, could marry a Heathen Greek! And such a backsleeding and downcoming after having been jined to one as has written such imms as the Bishop writ, which it is my preeveleege to know maistly by heart!'

O pestilential Glasgow Pharisaism and be bothered to you, you old fool!

In Malta I wander up and down the beautiful streets of Valetta and Senglea; and rejoice in the delightful heat and

the blue sky. I watch the thousands of little boats skimming across the harbour at sunset, and admire the activity and industry of the Maltese. I also drink very admirable small beer plenteously from pewter pipkinous pots and I may say with truth I am far happier than I might be or probably should be if still at sea!

By the by, what a fuss I see in the papers about the Art Show of the International Exhibition! Says I to myself I don't want no public praise nor blame nor nuffin: life is too short for such a lot of ugly anger!

Herewith a new sketch of the general appearance of a distinguished Landscape painter in Malta – his hair having taken to a violent excess of growth of late!

OF TRAVEL AND TITLES

Corfu, 30 November 1862.

I only got your ancient and fishlike letter dated the 10th, three days ago – I myself having only arrived here on the

23rd. I didn't go pretty straight to Corfu – au contraire, the road being broken up by torrents near Nice, I was obliged to go in a steamer to Genoa.

There was such a fat Cardinal on board and didn't I get a likeness of him under the table! Then I went to Ancona, but the Italian boats were postponed for a month, and so I had to wait for the small Trieste boat, which, coming, could not start for bad weather. Now I can't write consecutively for phits of coffin . . .

Sometimes I think the titles here are really very absurd. Take a list:

Sir Philotheros and Lady Damaschino
Sir Themistocles and Lady Zambelli
Sir Demetrius and Lady Curcumell
Sir Plato and Lady Platides,
Sir Karalambos and Lady Flamburiani
Sir Christopheros and Lady Kalikopolos Biletti Bizi

After which last nothing but Sir Agrios and Lady Polugorilloforos is to be expected! But this same list sets forth a love of title in these people – and indeed they are vain!

Of society – more another thyme. Of balls – of moons – of fish and other vegetables – and of all future and past events as things my be.

I have got a piano. Also a carpet. Also a tame redbreast: also a hearthrug and two doormats!

P.s. Here we hear that Mr. Gladstone is the favourite to be elected! I shall write to Mr. G. and ask him to make me 'Painter Laureate' and Grand Peripatetic Ass and Boshproducing Luminary – forthwith!

THE AUNT OF THE GIRL OF MAJORCA

Corfu, 11 January 1863.

O my eyes and little convulvuluses! If here isn't a letter sent by the Lord High a come from you!

Bye the bye, talking of fools, there is an old man here – partly so by nature and partly by drink – a seafaring man who has formerly been in the Balaeric Isles. He has taken a kind of monomaniac fancy to my *Nonsense Book* and declares that he knew personally the Aunt of the Girl of Majorca!

I hear it is more than humanity can bear to hear him point out how exactly like she is – and how she used to jump the walls in Majorca with flying leaps!!!

You vast owly Mortle! Why haven't you said on what day the marriage of yourself and Lady Waldegrave of which I 'ear is to be? Confound it – nor where it is to take place. Do tell me all . . .

I rejoice to state that the pictures I am doing – ten and 12 guinea ones – seem much liked. Nevertheless, reddy tin is scarce and bills abound.

Nonsense issues from me at times – to make a new book next year. The weather is at present lovely and the views over the harbour are of the most clipfombious and ompsiquillious nature . . . But here's somebod a nokking at the dolorous door. I must stop.

HEAD OVER HEELS AND OTHER JOYS

Corfu, 1 February 1863.

On the 30th ult. (which don't mean ultramarine but ultimo) came yours of the 19th confirming what I had read that your marriage *did* take place. Sir H. Storks, whom I met out walking yesterday said, 'If he is as happy as his friends wish him, he will be extremely so!'

Being a Lord High Commissioner, I did not slap him on the shoulder and say, 'Well said, old cove!' – though I wished to do so. I suppose you to be walking about on your head, or at least turning over and over, starfish fashion!

Meanwhile, my dear boy, I wish you and 'Mrs. Fortescue' every happiness and as long a lease of it as may be. And live as quietly as you can – rank and position permitting; for, as you know I think, in inward quietness lies greatest happiness.

The winter seems all gone for the present – though the Equal-noxious gales will doubtless come in disgustable force . . . I still lead the same quiet life, dining at the De Vere's or Palace on Sundays, and on Tuesdays somewhere or other; one or other of the garrison officers dining with me on Thursdays.

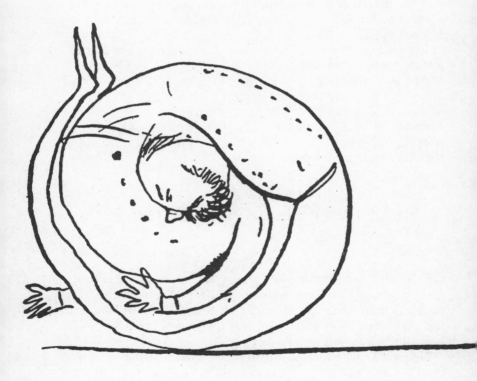

O child! Write! I can't any more. Nevertheless give my love to 'Mrs. Forescue'. I am collapsing with laughter and must go and bounce chords on the piano.

A NEMPTYSTUMMAK IS A BAD THING!

Corfu, 8 February 1863.

Your letter of the 30th delighted me extremely – you seem so thund'ring happy! I'm glad my Lady makes you get up early and take oss exercise. The plan of the 12 o'clock breakfast seems good: only take some coffee early or something – a nemptystummak is a bad thing. (Old Chevalier Kestner once said – calling out to someone in the street – 'Come and breakfast with me tomorrow: not a teapot but a forkëd collation!')

I was, however, much amused when I read that bit of your letter, because the evening before I heard a man – after growling at all 'Greeks' with the contemptuous annoyance of an Anglo-Saxon – speak as bitterly as he could of a nice young English officer married to a nice Greek girl as 'ceasing to be English entirely and becoming Greek altogether.'

'But how?' said I. And after obliging the man to confess that the Captain was as good tempered, as attentive to his duties, as fond of exercises, as regular at church, and so on, as before he married, the man began to get cross.

And at last he grumbled out, 'Well, then, I'll tell you what he does! He breakfasts à la fourchette at 11 or 12. And if you can say a man is an Englishman who does *that* – the devil's in it!'

My watercolour drawings are now all done but two – a really remarkable spot of energy: though by reason of sitting still and poking to see them, my neck has grown longer and my body fatter and I am like to this: –

My plans for the future are still unsettled. I think I shall pantechnichize for a good long time – and go about wandering, as it were, like a tailless baboon.

Athens does not appear to me to be a bad place to stick
in. I can't tell yet, but I think this year will see a change in
my life, if so be I live – for I don't look to do that very
long . . .

I wish you both as much happiness as you can gobble,
and am greatly rejoiced at your condition. Yours
absoquoxiously and full of blomphious and umpsidixious
congratulations.

'THE APERIENT GALSHIP OF ENGLISHWOMAN'

Ancona, 8 June 1863.

You see I am on my way so far, and I suppose I may be in
England on Friday and in town on Saturday. So that I shall
hope to see you and Lady Waldegrave on Sunday.

I have wearied awfully of the sea voyage – and do so
more and more. Perhaps the whole stagnation of a week or
more – besides the actual physical nuisance – makes me
determined to put an end to his double 'journey of life'. But
where I must live, so as to live *only* in one place, I can't yet
decide.

The farther I go from Corfu, the more I look back to the
delight its beautiful quiet has so long given me, and I am by
no means approaching the filth and horror and noise of
London life with a becoming spirit.

Sitting next to the Captain of a German Frigate at dinner
on Thursday, the conversation turned to the good looks of
women. Said the officer to a subaltern:

'I do think the Englishwoman conserve her aperient
Galship longer than all the women: even as far as her
Antics.'

The subaltern withered with confusion at this till I
ventured to explain, 'The Englishwoman preserves her
appearance of youth longer than all women – even if she be
old!'

From The 'Lord High Bosh And Nonsense Producer'

Oxford Street, London, 6 September 1863.

I want you to write to Lord Palmerston to ask him to ask the Queen to ask the King of Greece to give me a 'place'. As I never asked anything of you before, I think I may rely on your doing this for me.

I wish the place to be created a-purpos for me, and the title to be 'Lord High Bosh and Nonsense Producer' with permission to wear a fool's cap (or mitre), three pounds of butter yearly and a little pig – and a small donkey to ride on. Please don't forget all this, as I have set my heart on it!

I have finished my third view yesterday, 17 now remaining and I should have begun the forth if a brute of an Irishman hadn't interrupted me!

I asked a servant girl here – as I was having a friend to dine and wished to have the wine cool – for some ice. But she thought I said, 'I want some *mice*!' and was seized with a great fear forthwith!

A JOURNEY INTO THE PAST . . .

Oxford Street, London, 14 September 1863.

Bye the bye, one of the oddest feelings I can remember to have encountered came to me by a circumstance last Monday. On the Sunday, I had gone to Highgate Cemetery to see my dear sister Anne's grave, and returning, perceived afar, that the old house I was born in (its gardens and paddocks were long ago destroyed by new roads and buildings) was advertised for sale as building materials – four houses to be raised on its site.

So, the following day, I went up there and went all over it. And I can assure you, the annihilation of time which seeing such early-known localities produced was curious, and made me afterwards thoughtful enough.

As I stood in various parts of the large, empty rooms, I could absolutely hear and see voices and persons and could – had I had a pen and ink and paper and the time – have written out months and years of life nearly 50 years ago, exactly and positively!

The old women who shewed me the house seemed horribly puzzled at my knowing all the odd closets and doors, etc: and received two shillings and sixpence with a mixture of pleasure and fear . . .

I must now go and finish the seventh lithograph – wo is me. This work is so filthy. I shall never be clean again.

When it is finished I shall sit 10 days in a warm water pot, covered with a covering – and receive my friends – thus:

A NINTIMATION

Corfu, 15 January 1864.

My flight it seems was by no means too soon. Yet, after seven months of darkness and filth you will all as usual talk about the 'climate of England' as the 'best in the world'! So God tempereth the wind to the shorn lamb: so the Esquimaux believes that train oil is before all food the most excellent!

My life here (barring blowing my nose and lying in bed ill) has been of the most regular order – and it is a grim fact that never more when I go hence can I look for similar – 'there is no joy but calm'. Having put by £300 – £9 a year for life is the result of all my labour – but *quâ* ready money, and the necessity of getting it by work, things are as they were before the fathers fell asleep . . .

The two or three months of hard writing before I left England have sickened me of pen and ink, and I shall henceforth write MUCH LESS than formerly. *Please to accept this as a nintimation or warning*!

P.s. I will go to church this afternoon to pray that your toes may not be frozen off, and that it may please God to shew you the sun once or twice in the next four months!

CUT ADRIFT FROM CORFU

Hotel de la Couronne, Athens, 8 April 1864.

I hope you got a letter from me just before I left Corfu – of which I am now cut adrift, though I cannot write the name without a sort of pang.

Nothing could be sadder or more painful and vexing than the latter days I passed there. Everyone either miserable for going away – or miserable at being left. While angry passions and suppressed violence were abundant.

The brutal old leader of the extreme radicals put forth – three days before I came off – the foulest pamphlet against England a man could read (dated, of course, prior to the explanatory discussion in the Houses of Parliament, though he knew very well doubtless that he was writing lies!)

You may judge of the tone of this letter when I tell you – besides that I touched on all the crimes, real and imputed, which have been considered English for centuries of history – that it's last words are, 'We Ionians thank you that you have left us our hands and tongues; with the one to write your infamy and the other to utter threefold curses on your head!'

I-Spying In Nice

Villa Canapa, Nice, 13 November 1864.

Finding part of this envelope written and stick-stamped, I shall send it on principle, as one should eat all that is in a dish if the food 'won't keep.'

I have had sent me here a sermon by Bishop Colenso of Cape Town published at Longman's and called *Abraham's Sacrifice* – very remarkable and good. The ravening fanatics who persecute this man are highly devil-inspired.

Will there now be a new edition of the *Bible* – the filthy, savage or burlesque-upon-the-Deity passages left out? Shall you set it on foot any the more than that Lord Derby is advertising an edition of blank-verso *Homer*? If you do you can call it:

THE NEW
ANTIBEASTLY ANTIBRUTAL ANTIBOSH
BIBLE
By the Rt. Hon. Chichester S. Fortescue

I will take ten copies!

Do you know Nice? It reminds me a good deal of St. Leonards, only the houses are more detached and in many instances stand in gardens. The Promenade des Anglais is altogether a long row of lodgings – with a really good broad walk above the shingly beach.

The sea is rather deadly stupid, as there is no opposite coast, nor islands, nor ships, nor nothing, and the landskip is bounded by, west the headlands of Antibes, and east, by the Castle Hill and Villa Franca point – pretty enough.

Royal and Imperial folk abound, and no one notices them nor they nobody. Only they say the Russians have spies abunjiant everywhere, which, as there was a tame Pole at one Hotel I was at, and a Russ at another, don't seem unlikely!

I am going to Church this morning – more because I don't like systematically shewing a determination to ignore all outward forms than for any other cause: but it is possible I shall be disgusted, possibly I shall not go again. As the clergy go on now, they seem in a fair way of having – as the Irish gentleman said – only the four F's for their admirers: Fanatics, Farisees, Faymales and Fools!

NICE AND DRY

Promenade des Anglais, Nice, 24 February 1865.

I was never in so dry a place as this in all my life!
When the little children cry, they cry dust and not tears.
There is some water in the sea, but not much.
All the wetnurses cease to be so immediately on arriving.
Dryden is the only book read.
The neighbourhood abounds with Dryads and Hammerdryads.
And weterinary surgeons are quite unknown!

It really is a queer place – Brighton and Belgravia and Baden by the Mediterranean. Odious to me in all respects but its magnificent winter climate.

Were I the possessor of a villa I could live delightedly; but to have one's only chance of exercise in a crowded promenade of swells – one year is enough of that!

AMONG THE MALTEASERS

Valetta, Malta, 13 April 1866.

Did I tell you of my visit to Oudesh, vulgarly called Gozo? It was a pleasant one, and with the aid of my servant I drew every bit of it, walking fifteen or twenty miles a day. Its coast scenery may truly be called pomskizillious and gromphibberous, being as no words can describe its magnificence.

I have also drawn all Malta – more because I happened to be there, and some work had to be done, than for any good it is likely to do me. My whole winter gains – £25 – must remain a melancholical reminiscence of the rocky island and its community.

Were I to ask a Military Cove if this climate on account of its dryness required him always to pour water down his gun before firing it, or a Naval one if he weighed anchor before he sailed or a week afterwards, I should be laughed at as a fool – yet many not much less silly questions have been asked me!

A FEARFUL CROWD OF AMERICANS

Cairo, 9 March 1867.

I came back from having safely performed the first half of

PALMYRA

my journey – viz: the Nile and Nubia – and found your
very kind letter and the payment of £100 which you have so
kindly lent me. I am a queer beast to have such friends.

In a few days I go to Memphis for a day or two to wind
up my Egyptian work and then I hope to start across what
is called the short desert for Gaza, Askalon and Ashod. And
if I chance to find a nosering of Delilah with Samson's hair
set in it, won't I pick it up?

Then, after a time and times and half a time at Jerusalem,
I trust to go to Nazareth; the Sea of Galilee; that City on the
hill which is the site of the cursed, cursive, concurrent pigs;
Endor, with or without a witch; and if possible Gilead and
Gerarh, and if possibler, Palmyra.

Nubia delighted me, it isn't a bit like Egypt, except that
there's a river in both. Sad, stern, uncompromising
landscape, dark ashy purple lines of hills, piles of granite
rocks, fringes of palm, and ever and anon astonishing ruins
of oldest temples: above all wonderful Abou Simbel which
took my breath away.

An 'American' or Montreal cousin was with me above
Luxor, but he was a fearful bore – of whom it is only
necessary to say that he whistled all day aloud and was
'disappointed' in Abou Simbel!

You can't imagine the extent of the American element in
travel here! They are as twenty-five to one English. They
go about in dozens and scores – one dragoman to so many –
and are a fearful race mostly.

One lot of sixteen, with whom was an acquaintance of
my own, came up by steamer, but outvoted my friend,

who desired to see the Temple of Abydos because 'it was Sunday and it was wrong to break the Sabbath and inspect a heathen church'.

Whereon the Parson who was one of the party preached three times that day, and my friend shut himself up in a rage! Would it be believed, the same lot, Parson and all, went on arriving at Assouan – on a *Sunday* evening – to see some of those poor women whose dances cannot be described, and who only dance them by threats and offers of large sums of money!

As all outer adornments of the person – except noserings and necklaces – are disposed with on these occasions, the swallowing of camels and straining at gnats is finely illustrated!

SOME TOE-TAL PUNS

Lewes, Sussex, 24 November 1867.

Life, my child, is a bore! I didn't write a note to you about your injured Toe as I had wished to do, in which I meant to have recommended you to study the book of *To*bit, and to drink a glass of *To*kay, but not too much for fear you should go down into *To*phet and there be burned like Tow.

You should also have been told to eat *To*matoes, by way of soothing your *To*martydom, and in a word I should have totally punned the matter bare and out and out. In the meantime, don't be careless about your foot, as toes are not to be trifled with.

I go early tomorrow by Hastings to Folkestone – to cross on Tuesday. And by Thursday I hope to be at Cannes . . .

A BATH-TIME VISITOR . . .

6, Roosent Onnoray, Cannes, 24 Febbirowerry 1868.

I 'remained confounded' – as my servant Giorgio says when
he is surprised – 'rimasto confuso' – by getting a letter from
you and my Lady at once just now from the peripatetic
postman, whom in the street near my new lodgings I met.

The postman greets me always with great enthusiasm and
respect – especially since after a week had passed without his
bringing any letters I said to him:

'Do you know *why* there are no letters? It is because it is
too cold in England to hold a pen in one's hand.'

'That is indeed terrible, Sir,' said he.

And now that a burst of letters have turned up, he says,
'Look, Sir, the cold is beginning to go! My God, how cold
it must have been out there!'

You ax about my plans: they are still at a scroobious,
dubious, doubtfulness. If the Duchess of Buccleuch, Lord
Dalhousie or Mr. Jackson the millionaire come to sweep off
£300 of my drawings, I should go off to finish my Palestine,
because that kind of life is more difficult as one has to look
at it and undertake it at fifty sixcally or fifty sevenically.

But if they – the above-named potentates – don't come
and buy, I must sneak back to England in May or June,
perhaps only running over to Corsica for a *Cornhill* paper or
separately illustrated bit of journal, which I am inclined to
set my wits to as – Athos, or a portion of the Nile, or
Philistine country, etc, etc: thus gradually oozing out all my
intellectual topographic bowels as a silkworm doth its
caterpillary silk . . .

By all the Devils in or out of Hell! Four hundred and
seventy-three cats at least are all at once making a ninfernal
row in the garden close to my window. Therefore being
mentally decompoged, I shall write no more. Adding only a
portrait of myself on stilts (which mode of progress, as
practised here, I mean to learn) and another drawing

illustrative of what really occurred here some weeks ago.

All these beastly rooms where I am, open to an open court on the street, and my servant said, 'Better you lock the doors master, all the people come in!'

But I don't mind what he said. And, lo, when sponging myself in the tub – bounce! the door opened and one of the old market women with fowls and eggs rushed in. In dismay at my Garden of Eden state, she shrieked, let the fowls and eggs fall, and ran off – and until help came there was I all open to the passing world!

your confectionately
Edward Lear

PELICAN PIE IN PARADISE

Portland Place, London, 16 August 1869.

My life here is truly odious-shocking. Of my 28 days in England, the first seven went in bustle, looking for a lodging, and roughing out a plan of work. Of the next 21 – twelve have gone in necessary visits, and the remaining time has gone utterly in hard writing – often over one hundred notes in the day – in arranging a subscription list.

So rest there is none! When shall we fold our wings and list to what the inner spirit says – there is no joy but calm? Never in this world, I fear – for I shall never get a large northlight studio to paint in.

Perhaps in the next eggzi stens you and I and my Lady may be able to sit for placid hours under a lotus tree, eating of ice creams and pelican pie, with our feet in a hazure coloured stream and with the birds and beasts of Paradise sporting around us.

I can't help laughing at my position at fifty-seven! And considering how my pictures of Corfu, Florence, Petra, etc are seen by thousands and not one commission coming from that fact, how plainly is it visible that the wise public only give commissions for pictures through the Press that tell the sheep to leap where others leap!

And are you to be made a pier as the papers say you are?
'And hoping that such fact may come to pass,
Forgive the maunderings of a d---d old Ass!'

By The Light Of Lucifer Matches . . .

San Remo, 31 July 1870.

I live the queerest solitary life, in company of seventy people. They are, many of them, very nice, but their hours don't suit me and I hate life unless I work away. The scenery here is a most remarkable English character as to greenness, but of course, the Halps is bigger.

I should certainly like, as I grow old (if I do at all) to work out and complete my topographic life and publish my journals illustrated – for after all, if a man does *anything* all his life and is not a dawdler, what he does *must* be worth something, even if only as a lesson in perseverence.

The Piedmontese are really charming people, so simple and kindly. Only I wish they weren't all counts. Who ever heard before of an omnibus stuffed quite full of counts (8) and two Marquises?

I must tell you that I have been at one time extremely ill this summer. It is as well that you should know that I am told that I have the same complaint of heart as my father died of quite suddenly. I have had advice upon it, and they say I may live *any* time if I don't run suddenly or go quickly up stairs – but that if I do I am pretty sure to drop morto.

There, that's enough and more than enough. If you can't read this, nor Milady either, cut it across diagonally and read it zigzag by the light of 482 lucifer matches!

CRICKET JAM

Villa Emily, San Remo, 13 September 1871.

I'm pretty well again just now – but very much aged of late: internal accident tells as I grow older. I got unwell at Botzen – Bellzebubbotzenhofe, as I called it, on account of its horrid row of bells and bustle – and have only been restored to comparatively decent comfort since I came back here to my native 'ome and hair.

The spring here was absolutely lovely and my new house and garden very nice and amusing.

If you come here directly, I can give you 3 figs and 2 bunches of grapes; but if later, I can only offer you 4 small potatoes, some olives, 5 tomatoes and a lot of castor oil berries. These if mashed up with some Crickets who have spongetaneously come to life in my cellar, may make a novel, if not nice or nutritious Jam or Jelly!

Talking of bosh, I have done another whole book of it: it is to be called *More Nonsense* and Bush brings it out at Xmas: it will have a portrait of me outside.

Give my kind remembrances to my Lady. Mind, if ever you, either or both, come by here (whenever this Ministry tumbles) and don't let me know, I will never speak to you again as sure as beetles is beetles.

P.s. I've a Noffer to go with a Neldest son (Lord Northbrook) to the East for six months – tin cart blanche.

A NEST IN A TREE

Villa Emily, San Remo, Xmas Day, 1871.

I wonder if you have been edified by my *More Nonsense*
which I find is enthusiastically received by the world in
general?

My garden is a great delight, and looking beautiful. Mice
are plentiful and so are green caterpillars. I am thinking of
experimenting on both these as objects of culinary
attraction.

Whether I shall come to England next year or knot is as
yet idden in the mists of the fewcher. My 'elth is tolerable,
but I am 60 next May, and feel growing old.

Going up and downstairs worries me, and I think of
marrying some domestic henbird and then of building a nest
in one of my olive trees, where I should only descend at
remote intervals during the rest of my life.

This is an orfle letter for stupidity, but there is no help for
it!

A Case Of Indy-Gestion

Villa Emily, San Remo, 24 November 1872.

I got as far as Suez on my planned visit to India, but the landscape painter does not purSuez eastern journey father.

I am afraid neither you nor Lady Waldegrave will have any Indy-ink or Indy-rubber brought by me from Indy as I promised, and a fit of Indy-gestion is all that remains to me of that Oriental bubble at present.

And even that trouble I believe is less caused by my Indy-proclivities than by my having foolishly eaten a piece of apple pudding yesterday evening!

I found much greater difficulty in getting on than I had expected; at that season every hole and corner of the outward steamers is crammed, and although they frequently have a few berths as far as Malta or even Brindisi, yet late comers to these places have prior rights, so that after waiting a week you find that at Suez the list is filled up.

It is a bore to have lost so much time and money, but as Lady Young used to observe, 'Crying over spilt milk is nonsense' and with the few years of life now before me, I avoid lamenting as far as I can do so.

Who Or What Is The Ahkond Of Swat?

Villa Emily, San Remo, 12 September 1873.

On returning home last night from a vexatious journey to Genoa and back, I found your nice letter of the 3rd. A letter of yours (though as I have often said I never expect you to write) is always a Nepok in my life, albeit I have of late seen loads of your handwriting, having had to overhaul and mostly destroy three large chestfuls or chestsfull of Letters. A dreary task, yet one that has its good as well as its gloomy side.

At the end of my task I came to two positive conclusions. First, owing to the number and variety of my correspondents, that every created human being capable of writing ever since the invention of letters must have written to me – with a few exceptions, perhaps, such as the prophet Ezekiel, Mary Queen of Scots and the Venerable Bede. Secondly, that either all my friends must be fools or mad; or, on the contrary, if they are not so, there must be more good qualities about this child than he ever gives or has given himself credit for possessing – else so vast and long continued a mass of kindness in all sorts of shapes could never have happened to him!

This place has changed wonderfully since I came, the two properties next more particularly. The house below is all let to Germans for six years, a Hotel and Pension: and the ground is all bescattered with horrid Germen, Gerwomen and Gerchildren! Then, above me, the poor Congreve villa is still more changed, and I seldom now see him whom I had found so delightful a companion.

As for the Sanremesi, they are laudable and admirable in this respect only – that they leave you alone, unless they can make anything out of you! And as they can't me, they accordingly *do* leave me alone and I therefore admire them!

The place is divided into two parties – stationary and progressive. The last lay themselves out to sell land, houses, milk, wood – everything to the 'Forestieri' and all are courteous and civil, but there is not the faintest sign or shadow of anybody's caring one farthing for us in reality. Nor am I speaking as an Englishman: for I have heard Italian officers, who had been quartered in all parts, agreeing perfectly as to the character of the *whole* of the Riviera Genoese.

'They open their hands to get money, but *never* spend it,' venture these officers. 'Two words are not in their Dictionary – Generosità and Ospitalità!'

Now do you call this a long letter or don't you? I shall

stick double postage on it and fill up the rest with some parodies I have been obliged to make, whereby to recall the Tennyson lines of my illustrations: beginning with these mysterious and beautiful verses:

1. Like the Wag who jumps at evening
   All along the sanded floor.
2. To watch the tipsy cripples on the beach,
   With topsy turvey signs of screamy play.
3. *Tom-Moory* Pathos – all things bare –
   With such a turkey! such a hen!
   And scrambling forms of distant men,
   O! – ain't you glad you were not there!
4. Delirious Bulldogs – echoing, calls
   My daughter – green as summer grass: –
   The long supine Plebian ass,
   The nasty crockery boring falls.
5. Spoonmeat at Bill Porter's in the Hall,
   With green pomegranates, and no end of Bass.

I hear you say, 'You dreadful old ass!' But then my dear child, if your friend is the author of the *Book of Nonsense*, what can you expect?

I also send a ridiculous effusion, which in some quarters delighteth: the Ahkond of Swat. Of which one has read in the papers, and some one wrote to me to ask, 'Who or what is he?' – to which I sent this reply . . .

THE AHKOND OF SWAT

1. Why, or when, or which, or what
   Or who, or where, is the Ahkond of Swat, – óh *WHÂT*
           Is the Ahkond of Swat?

   ———————

2. Is he tall or short, or dark or fair?
   Does he sit on a throne, or a sofa, or chair, – or *SQUAT*?
           The Ahkond of Swat!

   ———————

3. Is he wise or foolish, young or old?
   Does he drink his soup or his coffee cold – or *HOT?*
   The Ahkond of Swat!

---

4. Does he sing or whistle, jabber or talk,
   And when riding abroad does he gallop or walk, – or *TROT?*
   The Ahkond of Swat!

---

5. Does he wear a Turban, a Fez, or a Hat,
   Does he sleep on a mattress, a bed, or a mat, – or a *COT?*
   The Ahkond of Swat!

---

6. When he writes a copy in roundhand size
   Does he cross his T's and finish his I's – with a *DOT?*
   The Ahkond of Swat!

---

7. Can he write a letter concisely clear,
   Without splutter or speck or smudge or smear, – or *BLOT?*
   The Ahkond of Swat!

---

8. Do his people like him extremely well,
   Or do they whenever they can, rebel, – or *PLOT?*
   At the Ahkond of Swat!

---

9. If he catches them then, both old and young,
   Does he have them chopped in bits, or hung, – or *SHOT?*
   The Ahkond of Swat!

---

10. Do his people prig in the lanes and park,
    Or even at times when days are dark – *GAROTTE?*
    O Ahkond of Swat!

---

11. Does he study the wants of his own dominion
    Or doesn't he care for public opinion – a *JOT?*
    The Ahkond of Swat!

---

12. At night, if he suddenly screams and wakes,
    Do they bring him only a few small cakes – or a *LOT*?
    For the Ahkond of Swat!

---

13. Does he live upon Turnips, tea, or tripe?
    Does he like his shawls to be marked with a stripe, or a
    SPOT?
    The Ahkond of Swat!

---

14. To amuse his mind, do his people shew him
    Jugglers, or anyone's last new poem – or *WHAT*?
    The Ahkond of Swat!

---

15. Does he like to lie on his back in a boat,
    Like the Lady who lived in that Isle remote, – *SHALOTT*?
    The Ahkond of Swat!

---

16. Is he quiet, or always making a fuss?
    Is his steward a Swiss, a French, or a Russ, – or a *SCOT*?
    The Ahkond of Swat!

---

17. Does he like to sit by the calm blue wave?
    Or sleep and snore in a dark green cave, or a *GROT*?
    The Ahkond of Swat!

---

18. Does he drink small beer from a silver jug?
    Or a bowl or a glass or a cup or a mug, – or a *POT*?
    The Ahkond of Swat!

---

19. Does he beat his wife with a gold-topped pipe,
    When she lets the gooseberries grow too ripe, – or *ROT*?
    The Ahkond of Swat!

---

20. Does he wear a white tie when he dines with friends
    And tie it neat in a bow with ends, – or a *KNOT*?
    The Ahkond of Swat!

---

21. Does he like new cream? Does he hate veal pies?
    When he looks at the sun does he wink his eyes? – or *NOT*?
                        The Ahkond of Swat!

---

22. Does he teach his subjects to toast and bake? –
    Does he sail about in an Inland Lake, in a *YACHT*?
                        The Ahkond of Swat!

---

23. Does nobody know, or will no one declare
    Who or which or why or where, – or *WHAT*
                        Is the Ahkond of Swat?

P.s. The effective way to read the Ahkond of Swat is to go
quickly through the two verse lines, and then make a loud and
positive long stretch on the monosyllable – hot, trot, etc., etc.

INDIA AT LAST!

Darjeeling, Bengal, 24 January 1874.

I finally decided that after all to go to India for 18 months
might do me good and, living as I do, from hand to mouth,
I could not throw away the commissions I had for paintings
and drawings . . .
    Writing long letters in India is simply an impossibility, if
you are sight-seeing and moving about to places hundreds
of miles off. So all I can do is to send scraps of intelligence
to friends, and wait for days of more leisure.
    I had a rather uncomfortable and long voyage out to
Bombay, getting there on November 23, and by December
1 had joined the Viceregal party at Lucknow. It is needless
to say I met with every possible kindness from all there. But
it was horrid cold, and I have never dared count my toes
since, being sure I left some behind.
    I saw all Cawnpore and Benares (which delighted me)

and Dinapore. Altogether, I got drawings of the country quite characteristic and my old servant Giorgio being always invaluable as a constant help in all sorts of ways.

I passed three weeks at Calcutta in Government House, but as you may imagine, the life was by no means to my taste, seeing I can't bear lights nor hours nor sublimities. Add to these matters a bad accident from a sketching stool breaking down under me – and you will say I had not cause to be too lively!

I came up here (a nodious and tedious journey of seven days) on the 16th and have been fortunate in getting outlines of the immense Himalayan Mountains, Kinchinjunga – which I am to paint for the Viceroy – and two more.

The foregrounds of ferns are truly bunderful – only there are no apes and no parrots and no nothing alive, which vexes me . . .

FLUMPING IN THE GANGES

Simla, 24 April 1874.

O! Chichester, my Carlingford!
O! Parkinson, my Sam!
O SPQ, my Fortescue!
How awful glad I am!

For now you'll do no more hard work
Because by sudden pleasing-jerk
You're all at once a peer!
Whereby I cry, God Bless the Queen!
As was, and is, and still has been,
Yours ever, Edward Lear!

Your letter came last night up from Calcutta and greatly pleased me. I am sorry I can't write much now, but I had an envelope already written for you and hope to fill it later.

I hope I may live through the blazing hot journey and get to Bombay before the 12th, when sixty-tooth year ends, and I shall be 'going on 63'.

Since I wrote from Darjeeling I have been all up the Ganges to Allahabad, then to Agra, Gwalior, Bhurtpoor, Muttra, Brindabund and Dehli, where I stayed ten days a making Delhineations of the Dehlicate architecture as is all impressed on my mind as inDehlibly as the Dehliterious quality of the water of that city!

Then I went up to Saharanpore and Mussoorie and Dehra and Roorkee and the great Ganges Canal to Hurdwur where is a Nindoo festival on the first week in April whereat on jubilee years three millions of pilgrims are found. (There are but 200,000 this year – quite enough!)

All these devout and dirty people carry out their theory of attendance on Public Wash-up on a great scale – by flumping simultaneously into the Holy Gunga at sunrise on April 11 – Squash!

Next I came up here, where I have been lent a house and servants all for myself and old George. I hate being such a swell, but what is one among so many? Whereas you are now a pier of the Rem and I am still a dirty Landskipper!

BOMBAY FASHIONS

Poona, 12 June 1874.

At present I have come (very unwillingly) to an anchor for a period unknown – because all the world says it is impossible to travel in the 'Rains'!

Yesterday I got some tin cases made and soldered up no less than 560 drawings, large and small, besides 9 small sketchbooks and 4 journals. I am going about my work with a method, and anyhow you and Milady will allow I am a very energetic and frisky old cove . . .

In travelling in India, you have three modes open to you: Dawk Bungalows, Hotels and Private Hospitality. The first is what I by far prefer. The second, Hotel halts, is in 19 cases out of 20 odious and irritating: indeed I can only name three or four hotels as yet visited, out of dozens. Thirdly, you may have letters to people at stations, and if so, you will in almost all cases be received with the greatest kindness.

Yet you cannot be master of your time in a private house as you are in a Dawk Bungalow. You certainly may say to the Lady of the House, 'Maam, I want tea at 5 – a cold luncheon and wine to take out with me, and dinner precisely at 7, after which I shall go to bed and shan't speak to you!' But such a proceeding is repugnant to my way of thinking – and the result of my experience is that you can't do as you like in other people's dwellings . . .

All the Bombay world rushes here at this season, when Bombay itself becomes mouldy and wet, and Mahabuleshwar and Matheran are uninhabitable.

(Metheran, by the bye, has most probably been the original Eden – I don't mean the first Lord Auckland – but Paradise: at least the scriptural scantiness of the apparel worn by the natives seems to point to Adam and Eve as its originators.)

It might be well that you should make some public suggestion that so economic and picturesque an apparel may be brought into general use in England. To assist you in so praiseworthy a departure from modern habits, I add a portrait to which you can refer *ad lib* . . .

'THE KING OF LIARS'

Villa Emily, San Remo, 28 March 1875.

Yes, I did return from India some two months sooner than I had intended. I hurt myself in getting into a boat in Travancore, and lumbago followed the sprain so disagreeably and persistently that I could not stoop or bear any sudden movement. So therefore I had to pass Mangalore, Carwar and Goa without landing and had even to give up Elephanta and straight off from Bombay on January 12 arriving – a wonderfully fine passage – at Brindisi on the 27th. It is very provoking not to have seen twenty-five or twenty-six things I particulary desired to visit, yet even had I been well I could not have done all those before April.

I did *not* enjoy Ceylon: the climate is damp which I *hate*. It is always more or less wet, and though the vegetation is lovely, yet it is not more so than that of Malabar where the general scenery is fine.

Ceylon makes people who arrive there from England *scream*! But then I didn't come from England, and so was not astonished at all, nor did I find any interest in the place as compared with India.

Did you ever hear of a Colonel Pattle? Indian life is full of stories of his exaggerations and they call him 'Joot Singh' – The King of Liars!

Someone at a dinner was saying that on coming from America, the ship's company saw a man floating on a hencoop; and putting off a boat offered to take the individual in.

'No,' said he, 'I am simply crossing the Atlantic by way of experiment, and all I would ask is a box of lucifer matches, mine having got wet.'

Everyone yelled at this American's story, and said what a fib!

But Colonel Pattle, waxing angry, said, 'It is no fib – but truth. *I* was the man on the hencoop!'

And when someone said Peas couldn't be grown at such a part of India, the Colonel interrupted: 'On the contrary – I grew Peas of such size and robustness that a whole herd of the Government elephants which were lost for three weeks were found concealed in my Peas!'

P.s. There is so much vegetable luxuriance in Ceylon that even the marrow in peoples' bones is Vegetable marrow. My!

You must have a choice from my Indian drawings and

select one you like best. Perhaps you will like the one I made at Matheran showing scantily clad women!

I made my first essay at showing these scantily clothed females to three ladies with fear and trembling. All three looked in demure silence till one said, 'What very odd costumes!'

Then the second exclaimed, 'Rather no costume, I think!' And the third added, 'Ah! I always heard the naked people with brown skins were not at all indelicate!'

So I have now no further dread of the subject!

RIDING ON A PORPOISE!

Riverhead, 7 Oax, 26 September 1875.

This is only a wurbl message as it is to say goodbye to you and my lady, and I wish you both a appy Xmas. I have been very unwell lately – the damp having brought on Assma odiously. However, I have got pretty nearly clean off and am now on my way to Folkestone.

If the sea is very rough I mean to hire a prudent and pussillanimous porpoise and cross on his back! I suppose I shall get to San Remo early in October, old Giorgio having already arrived there to clean up and beautify the willer.

As for Sevenoaks, I was truly serene and happy with my dear friend Lushington's family and children, yet the 'turf' and 'fresh air' brought on asthma hideously and I found myself a bore – spite of all their kindness – because I had to beg for shut windows, or else I coughed like unto a coughy mill. Whereby and so and therefore I gradually felt – this of 1875 will be (if not my last) nearly my last visit to the land of my posteriors.

O my child – here is a gnat! Which, the window being open, is but gnatural. So I shuts up both vinder and letter, and goodbye!

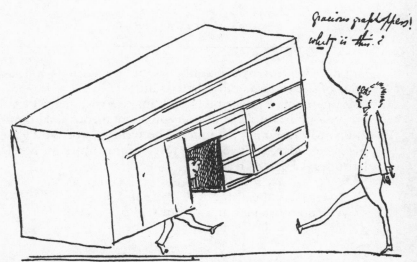

gracious grasshoppers! what is this!

please Sir it's a little table, as has come from Mr. Fortescue.

GERPERSONS AND OTHERS

Villa Emily, San Remo, 6 January 1876.

The weather has been simply Paradise from 3 October to 5 January – but now it is changed, coldy and wet. Yet I have no fires by day yet, and write this by an open window, Foss the cat on the ledge. Oranges and flowers in the garden magnificent . . .

Society slender. In fact, Sanremo is fast becoming less and less of an English colony since the French War which sent all the Germen and Gerwomen here. (Positively, there are now 80 in one hotel!) And it is a painful fact that many English ladies flee such hotels – the Germans, they say, spit at dinner-time and smoke all night! So the nationalities aloof-stand.

Meanwhile, the Germans are sent here simply to die! Twenty-three have died since November 1st, and all sent back to Germany – which I know so accurately about because W. Congreve, our Vice Consul, has to superintend and numerate these necropolitan derangements. W. Congreve and his sons, my next neighbours, are a blessing – but, as I said, of society generally there is little.

Remember, if ever you should make a rush here, I can put you up beautiful and feed you spontaneous-analogous.

P.s. My library is a winner! The writing table you gave me is considered the loveliest piece of furtniture in these latitudes – for which accept

       my gratitudes – and may you meet
     with beattitudes – whereon I'll
write no more platitudes – but will go to lumpshon
    with a clear conscience!

TOPSY TURVEY ART

Villa Emily, San Remo, 14 April 1877.

I am still living on from day to day. I work pretty hard all day, except on Weddlesdays when I have people to see my Vorx of hart – and when happily some drawings are now and then sold.

I wish my Lady could have seen the two large pictures of which my friend and admirer Sir Spencer Robinson says, 'There are no such pictures in England.' Others seem pleased with their paintings, too, but several bad accidents have happened to people injuring their brains from standing on their heads in an extasy of delight before these works of art!

What, however, *is* pleasant is this – that at no previous period of female English costume could ladies have so given way to their impulses of admiration without affronting the decencies and delicacies – whereas now they can postulate theirselves upside down with impunity, and no fear of petticoatical derangement!

THE ELLIPTICAL CHEMIST!

Villa Emily, San Remo, 28 October 1878.

Some people are older at sixty-seven than others, and I am one of those, though I am very thankful to say I am generally in good health. And the interest I have in my very beautiful garden is always a delight. I have also now a large library, and can lend a hundred or more volumes to invalids during the season.

My hair likewise is falling off, and I rejoice to think that the misery of hair cutting will soon cease! Morever I have lovely broad beans in April and May, and the Lushingtons come and stay with me, so that altogether I should be rather surprised if I am happier in Paradise than I am now.

By the bye, a Gent who bought one of my paintings recently was an 'Analytical Chemist' whatever that may be – and there is a lady here who deranges epitaphs as famously as Mrs. Malaprop.

'I hear,' quoth she, 'that the person who has taken the villa next door is an *epileptical* chemist.'

'Good heavens,' said her husband, 'what stuff you talk!'

'Well,' said the woman, 'you needn't be so sharp if one makes a mistake – of course, you know I meant an *Elliptical* Chemist!'

Monte Generoso nearby is quite the best place of the sort

I have known, the walks delightful and the views wonderful. You could see the flies walking up the Cathedral of Milan any afternoon. The thunder storms were a bore, though.

A queer little boy three or four years old at the Hotel had never heard thunder, and asked what the big drum was.

'The noise is made by God Almighty,' said his mother.

'My!' said the child, 'I didn't know he played on the Drum! What a big one it must be to be heard all the way down here!'

Another tale of children. Some years ago I called with Lady Davy at the home of Sir Charles Eardley and was met by the three little Eardleys.

'Papa is coming directly,' they informed us, 'we have been in his study and have blessed privileges.'

'What are those?' said Lady Davy.

'Blessed Privileges,' said the two girls again.

'But *what*? – can you tell me, little man' (to the brother).

'Yes,' quoth he, 'they are the tops of Papa's three eggs, and we three eat one apiece in his study!'

P.s. Ahkond of Swat would have left me all this ppproppprty, but he thought I was dead: so didn't. The mistake arose from someone officiously pointing out to him that King Lear died seven centuries ago, and that the poem referred to one of the Ahkond's predecessors!

RIVIERA GEOGRAPHY

Villa Emily, San Remo, 19 October 1879.

The loneliness of this place now is frightful to me – there is no possibility of intellectual conversation with Riviera people. They only think of money, money, money.

I don't believe there are six of the town people who wouldn't believe me if I told them that Calcutta was inside Madras, and both of the cities in Bombay, with Australia, Japan and Jamaica all distinctly seen from the shore!

However, as you have more trouble than I since the sudden death of my Lady, I will try to be a good boy and as cheerful as possible . . . My thoughts are with you, dear friend.

THE GREAT MARMALADE TRAGEDY

Villa Emily, San Remo, 30 March 1880.

Your letter from Veytaud, which came yesterday morning, was a relief, as I had fully expected to have worse news instead of better news. I sent your letter to Constance and she and Eddie are coming to lunch with me today, which is very amiable of them. We are to have a Pilaff, a roast fowl and some squints with pears.

I regret to state that they never got any marmalade, for the porter of the *Londres* to whom was committed the potly perquisite, declared that the pot fell down and was broken and the contents lost: a catastrophy which may or may not have occurred.

I am also sorry to tell you that there is no longer any hope of my being able to forward to England that old gentleman who watched over my peas and Beans – for two nights ago the wind blew him down and his head and one leg came off, so that he is not in a condition to travel . . .

P.s (Dated April Phiffth, 1880) As for the pot of marmalade, Giorgio jumped to the same conclusion as yourself: viz – that if the marmalade did not lie on the ground, the Porter did!

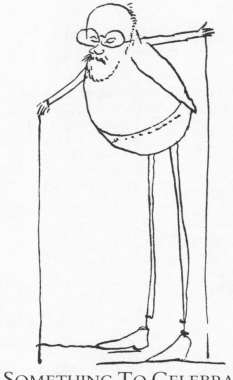

SOMETHING TO CELEBRATE

Villa Tennyson, San Remo, 31 October 1881.

I wish to inform you of the fax that I am settled in my new abode. It has taken longer than I thought and Giorgio once said to me, 'The new House he go like a tortoise!'

Something else my good old servant said a few days ago would also – had you been here – have probably caused you to have half fallen off your chair laughing as I nearly did. For he came in and standing before me said, 'Master, I come say something.'

I thought it some fresh bother about his family and said, 'Very well, Giorgio, say on.'

'Master, I think you take more wine than be is good for you!' said G.

I found that he had discovered that the shop Marsala I have been drinking to be half spirits! Yet, as I had drunk it with Appollinaris, I did not find that out. He had suspected it by its smell – and putting a spoonful near the fire, it all flared up!

So I merely take one glass at lunch in one of his wonderfully good puddings – bread or rice (my whole luncheon) – and at 6.30 I have a glass or two of red wine of the country.

This diet has evidently agreed with me, and I have not only got generally better, but have slept well, too!

THE PRIVY SEAL

Villa Tennyson, San Remo, 30 March 1882.

There have been some absurd rumours about Queen Victoria coming here, and the other day over a hundred owly fools came up and stood all about my gate for more than an hour! But on finding that no Queen came, went away gnashing their hair and tearing their teeth.

I hope if H.M. does come, I shall be told of the future event before it comes to pass, as it would not be pretty to be caught in old slippers and shirt sleeves. I dislike contact with Royalty as you know; being a dirty landscape painter apt only to speak his thoughts and not to conceal them.

The other day when someone said, 'Why do you keep your garden locked?' Says I: 'To keep out beastly German bands and odious wandering Germans in general.'

Says my friend, 'If the Queen comes to your gallery, you had better not say that sort of thing.'

Says I – I won't if I can help it . . .

I suppose that, connected as you are with Ireland, and naturally cognizant with Irish politics, you have more on your hands and in your head than the Office of Privy Seal generally has to attend to. Nevertheless, I have never had a clear idea of what the Privy Seal's work really is: and my last notion is that you have continually to superintend seal

Ye privy . seal

catching all round the Scotch and English coasts, in order to secure a government monopoly of seal skin and seal calves . . .

Sometime back when I thought you were coming out here I wrote the enclosed in Italian for your bemusement:

A curious circumstance and one worthy of note must also be recorded because a similar fact is not found in the Ceremonies of any other Royal Court whatsoever.

Before the guests go to their rooms – after the Queen has left the Gallery – the President of the Privy Council is seen entering, followed by ten servants in livery. Not, however, as President, but as Guardian of the Great Seal – a post of the greatest importance and significance, and only given to the most trustworthy, learned, clever and amiable gentleman of the Court.

By the side of the Lord Guardian, and held by him by means of a chain, the Seal – which has no feet – makes its progress all through the Gallery and is, so to speak, taken to make the acquaintance of all the guests.

One cannot well describe the motion of this enormous animal, as Italian is lacking in words that adequately translate 'Wallop' or 'Flump' – verbs that well suit its motion, but are unknown to us Italians. Many ladies are a good deal frightened the first time that they see the Great

Seal, but they are strictly forbidden to scream.

When it has been all round the Gallery, this amiable beast withdraws again with a 'Wallop-flump' with the Lord Guardian. And before retiring, the latter gives the Seal more than 37 pounds of macaroni, 18 bottles of champagne, 2 beefsteaks and a ball of scarlet worsted – all of which are brought by 10 servants in livery!

I'M GLAD I'M NOT A CENTIPEDE!

Villa Tennyson, San Remo, 23 December 1883.

Thank the Lord that you are not a Centipede! A bust of gratitude I feel every Sunday morning because on that day happens the weekly cutting of toenails and general arrangement of toes. And if that is a bore with ten toes, what would it have been if it had been the will of Heaven to make us with a hundred feet, instead of only two – i.e. with five hundred toenails!

It has been before now a subject of placid reflection and conjecture to me as to whether Sovereigns, Princes, Dukes and even Peers generally cut their toe nails. It is useless to think of asking hereditary Peery individuals about this as they are brought up to recognise such facts as so to speak impersonal and beyond remark. But it is possible that I may find out some day if you will continue this odious annoyance after you are entitled to wear a coronet!

As regards myself and my own health, I cannot tell you much good. I had a bad fit or attack after I wrote last and fell – happily – in the garden, remaining insensible for some time. Since then I have had no other similar shock, but only threatenings of paralysis. I rarely go out beyond my own villa, and am quite prepared for a sudden departure at any time – regretting only that I cannot leave, as I had with justice hoped to do, my wordly affairs in order.

P.s. Concerning godsons. One Mr. Jones here had this

announcement made to him by a waiter, 'Sir, a gentleman wishes to see you. He says he is the Son of God belonging to your friend Mr. Smith!!'

A PHILOPOBÓSTROGOTRÓBBICLE QUESTION

Villa Tennyson, San Remo, 21 January 1884.

If you will start off at once so as to get here while this fine weather lasts, you shall have my two volumes of Lodge – if you are a good boy – to read all day. Which you can do in your own room, looking out on the sounding syllabub sea and the obvious octagonal ocean.

And, bye and bye, I will alter my garden so as to give room for a waterspouty small aqueous circular basin, in which, in remembrance of you, a live Phoca shall ever dwell, and I will observe it from the brink!

I was interested in your remarks on being left alone since milady's death. The longer I live the more I think I perceive the spaces of this life to be inexpressibly trivial and small, and that, if there be a life beyond this, our present existence is merely a trifle in comparison with what may be beyond. And that there is a life beyond this it seems to me the greatest of absurdities to deny, or even doubt of.

As a rule I avoid writing on Poltix, but now and then I cannot help alluding to them: for the present I shall only say, in the remarkable words of a Mrs. Malaprop here, 'The present Government is one of vaccination and no policy; nor does it ever act with derision until it is obliged to do so by some dreadful Cataplasm!'

> When 'Grand Old Men' persist in folly
> In slaughtering men and chopping trees,
> What art can soothe the melancholy
> Of those whom futile 'statesmen' tease?
> The only way their wrath to cover
> To let mankind know who's to blame-o
> Is first to rush by train to Dover
> And then straight onward to Sanremo!

I have often seen in lists of dinners, 'Cabinet Puddings' named. Now what I have a painful curiosity to know is whether all you Cabinet Ministers have such a pudding placed before you at Cabinet Councils and if Mr. Gladstone has a huge big one at the head of the table?

Respond – this being an important philopobóstrogotróbbicle question . . .

THE LIFE OF UNCLE ARLEY

Villa Tennyson, San Remo, 4 June 1884.

Having a notion that you have a little more leisure while you are at Balmoral (as I see by the papers you are about to be) than when you are in London, I shall send you a few lines just to let you know how your aged friend goes on.

> O my aged Uncle Arley!
> Sitting on a heap of Barley
> Through the silent hours of night!
> On his nose their sate a cricket –

In his hat a railway ticket –
But his shoes were far too tight!
Too! Too!
　　　far too tight!

By the 15th May I was just able to get away from here on my journey of discovery. I was frightfully pulled down by my illness – with swollen feet and unable to walk. But Giorgio's youngest son, Dimitri, continually pulled me into and out of Railway carriages like a sack of hay. So by dint of pluck and patience I got to Vicenza and to Recoaro, where I have taken rooms for eight or ten weeks.

A thunderbolt happened recently in Christie's having at the last moment declared that they had no room or time left for my sale of pictures, so all are gone to Foords. Please do what you can to make my Eggzibition known. Some of the work there is of the best I have done, I think.

In the meantime I rise now at 4.30 and after 6 work at the never finished Athos, and the equally big Bavella, and the infinitely bigger Enoch Arden . . .

I daresay you have plenty to do, so I shall not write any more. I often wish you were here.

ARCHBISHOP LEAR!

Villa Tennyson, San Remo, 30 April 1885.

You must have been glad to get back to England, for I know Court life is not to your taste – though a duty. As for me, I never could have mastered it even in that light. For one day, after long repression of feeling, I should suddenly have jumped all round the room on one leg – or have thrown a hot potato up to the ceiling – either of which acts would possibly have ruined my 'career' as G.F.B. used to say.

You are certainly a wonderful cove – if so be a Cabinet

Minister is a cove – for writing so much and so kindly to this 'dirty Landscape painter', who not seldom repents of his violent writing to a 'statesman with a well-balanced mind', as I truly believe you to be.

Should you be injuiced, by contemplating the remarkable development of my 'Political knowledge and aspirations' to offer me some lucrative place under Government, be assured that I will take nothing but the Chancellor of Exchequership or the Archbishoprick of Canterbury!

Various people bother me to publish my Autobiography, but at present I shan't. Some of the notes written in years when I used to drive for days on the Campagna with Lady Davy are funny enough; as are others not in that category.

Now if you've got so far, you've read enough.
Ps.
And this is certain; if so be
You could just now my garden see,
The aspic of my flowers so bright
Would make you shudder with delight!

And if you voz to see my roziz
As is a boon to all men's noziz
You'd fall upon your back and scream –
'O Lawk! O Criky! It's a dream!'

BAKED BAROMETERS AND STEWED THERMOMETERS

Villa Tennyson, San Remo, 19 February 1886.

I am very sorry to hear you are so poorly. As for myself I am sitting up today for the first time. I go with medicine every three hours and the cough – which has shaken off one of my toes, two teeth and three whiskers – is, thank God, somewhat diminished.

But I am still very ill and have only till today been able to leave my bed by being lifted out of it and rolled into a chair. It is a great blessing that the sun is always so bright.

I continue to miss your visits extremely, but could not wish you to be here now, for though the sun is hotter, the wind is colder.

Hassall, my Doctor, irritates me by his d---d Thermometers and Barometers. As if I couldn't tell when an East wind cuts me in half – spite of the Thermometer! – by reason of sunshine being ever so high.

I told him just now that I had ordered a baked Barometer for dinner, and two Thermometers stewed in treacle for supper!

NOTHING TO SAY!

Villa Tennyson, San Remo, 10 December 1886.

Once at a village prayer meeting, this conversation took place.
First old woman, 'Say something!'
Second old woman. Ditto. 'What shall I say?'
First old woman. Ditto. 'How can I tell?'
Second old woman. Ditto. 'There is nothing to say!'

Both. 'Say it then at once!'

I send this card, but having nothing to say but that I am not worse, perhaps rather better at times, but still quite disabled by rheumatism in arm and leg – the right.

He only said, 'I'm very weary. The rheumatiz, he said. He said, it's awfull dull and dreary. I think I'll go to bed.'

PIGEON CLOCKS

Villa Tennyson, San Remo, 18 June 1887.

You will be glad to hear I am considerably better. At 7 a.m. today I walked nearly round all the garden, which for flowers in bloom is now a glorious sight.

I have ten pigeons which are a glorious diversion, though they are beginning to be rather impudent and aggressive. Their punctuality as to their sitting on their eggs and vice versa I never knew of before. The males and females take their turns EXACTLY every two hours.

My servant says he believe they have little watches under their wings, and that they wind them up at sunset, 8 p.m., standing on one foot and holding the watch in the other!

ADIEU . . .

Villa Tennyson, San Remo, 10 November 1887.

I should like to know how you are going on. I have gone back a good deal lately, but am better today than for three days past when I had a nasty fall.

The pains in my side are, says Hassall, caused by Champagne! So he has prohibited my drinking any more at present – a great and ridiculous bore, inasmuch as Frank Lushington has just sent me 30 bottles as a present. And moreover I detest cognac and water . . .

Did you see the notice about my works in *The Spectator* of October 27? Vere nice indeed . . .

Write soon, if only a card.

Yours affectionately,

EDWARD LEAR

This was Edward Lear's last letter to his friend. He died quietly at the Villa Tennyson on January 29 1888. 'The Old Landskipper' had finally come to rest. (The Spectator item which so delighted Lear in his final hours appears at the end of this book.)

THREE

SCRIBBLEBIBBLES

n his letters to his various friends and corre-
spondents, Lear delighted in introducing
throw-away lines and asides in which he
drew amusing comparisons between the
most unlikely people, animals and objects.
Though he had no particular term to describe
these wry comments, the word 'Scribblebibble', which he
coined in December 1859 to describe a series of random
reflections and observations, seems to me to perfectly fit these
unique 'Learisms'.

I have therefore extracted the following 'Scribblebibbles'
from a wide cross-section of his letters spanning the years
from 1851 to the closing year of his life. Though Lear himself
probably had no intention that they should be collected, there
could surely be no more suitable manner to do so than in the
alphabetical order which now follows.

A

These facts I only came upon granulously, as it were, grain
by grain – as the ANT said when he picked up the bushel of
corn slowly! (1862)

B

I should also like to see a little more of other places yet, but
that must be as it may – as the BOY said when they told
him he mustn't swallow the mustard pot and sugar tongs!
(1870)

C

After all one has much to be thankful for – as the
CENTIPEDE said when the rat bit off ninety-seven of his
hundred legs! (1882)

I must close this – as the CYCLOPSES used to say of
their one eye! (1882)

I am partly dressed – as the CUCUMBER said when oil
and vinegar were poured over him: salt and pepper being
omitted! (1886)

D

What is the use of all these revolutions which lead to
nothing? – as the DISPLEASED TURNSPIT said to an
Angry Cookmaid! (1865)

E

Better than a poke in the eye with a sharp stick – as the
ELEPHANT said to the mouse! (1873)

F

But enough of this – as the FROG said angrily to the Lizard
who averred that he was neither fish nor beast after his tail
fell off! (1884)

G

What do I know? – as the GNAT said when the
Hippopotamus asked him what the Moon was made of!
(1882)

H

You see – as the little HADDOCK said in the Pacific, I am
all at sea! (1864)

I

I don't see any particular reason for doubting its success by
little and little – as the IRISHMAN said when he threw the
gunpowder into the fire! (1884)

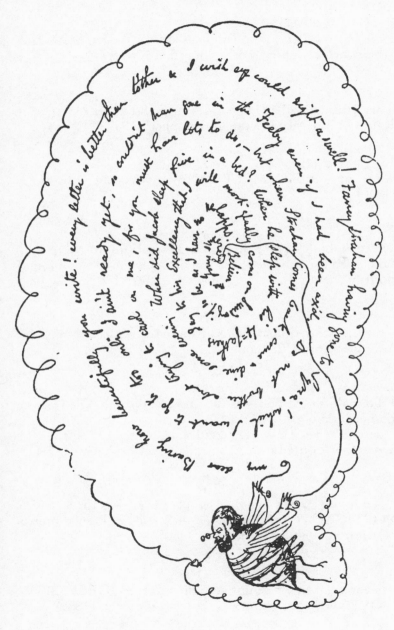

J

I still have something to laugh about – as the JACKAL said when one of his ears was bitten off! (1869)

K

This letter will all be in jumps – as the fidgetty KANGAROO said to the grasshopper! (1882)

L

Cheer up – as the LIMPET said to the Weeping Willow! (1860)

M

On the whole – as the morbid and mucilaginous MONKEY said when he climbed to the top of the Palm-tree and found no fruit there – one can't depend on dates! (1882)

N

This is a nextra gnoat along of a nun4seen stircumstance – as I said to myself! (1866)

O

I did it all for the best – as the OLD SOW said when she sat on her little pigs! (1851)
   I am in a very unsettled condition – as the OYSTER said when they poured melted butter all over his back! (1871)

P

'E'en in our hashes live their wonted fires' – as the POETICAL COOK said when they said her hashed mutton was not hot enough! (1884)

Q

I never seem to get things straight – as the QUEER OLD COVE said when he turned the wrong corner! (1859)

R

All very strange and upside down – as the RAT said when he bit off his grandmother's tail, having mistaken it for a straw! (1870)

S

So I must e'en turn over another stone – as the SANDPIPER said when he was a looking for vermicules! (1848)

My thread is broken – as the SPIDER said to the housemaid! (1862)

I have no energy – said the SHRIMP who had swallowed a Norfolk Dumpling! (1866)

My thread is broken – as the SPIDER said to the housemaid! (1862)

T

I'll make up for lost time – as the TADPOLE said when he lost his tail and found he could jump about! (1860)

Concentrate your ideas if you want to do anything well, and don't run about – as the TORTOISE said to the Armadillo! (1863)

U

It never rains but it soaks you – as the UMBRELLA said when turned inside out! (1877)

V

It's hard to pick and choose – as the VULTURE said when the lordly Lion stole his meal! (1880)

W

I must stop now – as the WATCH said when the little boy filled it full of treacle (1884)

XYZ

There are no XYZs – as the EDITOR said after all his researches! (1987)

FOUR

The Wearisome Old Man Of Vetere

And Other Gleanings from the Journals
of a 'Dirty Landscape Painter'

s Lear mentioned in one of his letters to For-
tescue, he kept detailed journals during his
painting trips and later published three
volumes of these based on his tours of
Southern Calabria (now southern Italy),
Albania (as well as part of Greece) and
Corsica. These three works provide an entertaining account of
his wanderings and the places he visited and painted or
sketched, as well as offering a number of pen-portraits of some
of the quite extraordinary local people he met and who, the
reader will soon realise, were another source of inspiration for
his nonsense.

Lear frequently referred to himself as a 'dirty Landscape
Painter' and the origin of this curious expression has been
explained by Angus Davidson in his biography. 'It was on one
of these tours,' he says, 'that Lear overheard a conversation
between two young Englishmen in the inn where he was
staying. "I say, Dick, do you know what that fellow is that we
were talking to last night?" "No." "Why, he's nothing but a
d---d dirty landscape-painter!" Lear's fancy was greatly

tickled by this description of himself, and he adopted it as a kind of professional title – "Edward Lear, Dirty Landscape Painter".'

In the pages which follow I have selected some of the most amusing of the portraits which appeared in the three journals which are now, not surprisingly, of considerable rarity, never having been republished in well over one hundred years. The extracts appear chronologically and are taken, respectively, from *Journals of A Landscape Painter in Southern Calabria* (written in 1847 and first published by Richard Bentley in 1852), *Journals of a Landscape Painter in Albania & Illyria* (written in 1848 and also published by Bentley, in 1851) and *Journal of a Landscape Painter in Corsica* (written in 1868 and published by Robert Bush in 1870).

Travel in Lear's day was nothing like the highly sophisticated business it is today, of course. It was mostly undertaken on foot or on the back of a mule, and there were few decent roads and even fewer hotels and hostelries. And though the artist usually carried letters of introduction from one place to another, he was often not quite sure where he and Giorgio were going to lay their heads down each evening! Something of the tribulations of travel in the middle years of the last century may be judged from these evocative lines which Lear wrote in July 1847: 'The greatest penance of this roving life is the state of exhaustion and weariness in which you arrive at your evening abode; and as you feel very properly obliged to play the polite guest for a time to your entertainers, the wrestling between a sense of duty and an oppressive inclination to sleep is most painful. The good people, too, persist in delaying supper (in order that they may provide a good one) till you are reduced (ere it comes) to a state of torture and despair, in the protracted struggle between Hunger, Morpheus and Civility!'

I

SOUTHERN CALABRIA

(1847)

CICCO THE DOGO-MAN

We have engaged a muleteer for an indefinite time for our tour. The expense for both guide and quadruped being six carlini daily – and if we send him back from any point of our journey it was agreed that his expenses should be defrayed until he reached Reggio.

Our man, a grave, tall fellow of more than fifty years of age, and with a good expression of countenance, was called Cicco. We explained to him that our plan was to do always just as we pleased – going straight ahead or stopping to sketch, without reference to any law but our own pleasure. To which he replied by a short sentence ending with, 'Dogo: dighi, doghi, daghi, da!' – a collection of sounds of frequent recurrence in Calabrese lingo, and the only definite portion of that speech we could never perfectly master! What the 'Dogo' was we never knew, though it was an object of our keenest search throughout the tour to ascertain if it were animal, mineral or vegetable!

Afterwards, by constant habit, we arranged a sort of conversational communication with friend Ciccio, but we never got on well unless we said, 'Dogi si!' or 'Dogo no!' several times as an *ad libitum* appoggiatura, winding up with 'Dighi, doghi, daghi, da!' which seemed to set all right!

29 July 1847.

BOILED SILKWORM AND MOTH TARTS

Don Domenico Musitani, the chief man of the place, to whom the never-failing care of the Consigliere da Nava had recommended us, was sitting in the Piazza – an obese and taciturn man, who read the introductory letter and forthwith took us to his house, which, among many unpleasing recollections, will certainly ever rank as one of the most disagreeable.

Life in these regions of natural magnificence is full of vivid contrasts. The golden abstract visions of the hanging woods and crags were suddenly opposed to the realities of Don D. Musitani's rooms, which were so full of silkworms as to be beyond measure disgusting. To the cultivation of this domestic creature all Staiti is devoted; yellow cocoons in immense heaps are piled up in every possible place, and the atmosphere may be conceived rather than described. Almost did we repent of ever having come into these Calabrian lands!

After the usual refreshment of snow and wine, we waited wearily for supper, at times replying to the interrogations of our host on the subject of the productions of Inghilterra, and right glad were we when dismissed to what rest might be found in couches apparently clean, though odious from the silkworms all around them. But necessity as well as poverty makes the traveller acquainted with strange bedfellows!

Long before daylight a troop of pigeons came into our room through the ill-shut door, and after them followed fowls, then dogs – all of which visitors we rejoiced to leave and were soon exploring the town. Staiti has its full share of Calabrian mystery in its buildings, caves and rocks, and employed our pencils far and near till noon, when we returned to our hosts to find dinner laid out in one of the bedrooms, all among the silkworms as before. Nor did the annoyance of a tribe of spoiled children and barking dogs add charms to the meal.

But the 'vermi di seta' were our chief horror; and so completely did silkworms seem the life and air, end and material, of all Staiti, that we felt more than half sure, on contemplating three or four suspicious-looking dishes, that those interesting lepidoptera formed a great part of the ground work of our banquet – silkworms (plain boiled), stewed chrysalis and moth tart!

4 August 1847.

The Remarkable Count Garrolo!

The Conte was a most good natured and fussy little man, excessively consequential and self-satisfied, but kind withal, and talking and bustling in the most breathless haste, quoting Greek and Latin, hinting at antiquities and all kinds of dim lore and obscure science, rushing about, ordering his two domestics to and fro, explaining, apologising and welcoming, without the least cessation.

He had come from a villa, he told us, a villetta, a vigna – an old property of the family – Giovanni Garrolo, Gasparo

Garrolo, Luca Garrolo, Stefano Garrolo – he had come just
now, this very minute. He had come on a mule, on two
mules, with the Contessa, the amiable Contessa, he had
come slowly – pian, pian, piano, piano, piano – for the
Contessa expected to be confined today – perhaps today –
he hoped not! He would like us to be acquainted with her;
her name was Serafina; she was intellectual and charming;
the mules had never stumbled; he had put on the crimson-
velvet housings, a gilt coronet embossed, Garrolo, Garrolo,
Garrolo, Garrolo, in all four corners; he had read the
Contessa an ode to ancient Locris all along the road, it
amused her, a Latin ode; the Contessa enjoyed Latin; the
Contessa had had six children, all in Paradise, great loss, but
all for the best; would we have some snow and wine?

Bring some snow, bring some wine, he commanded
without stopping. He would read us a page, two pages,
three – Locri Opuntii, Locris Epizephyrii, Normans,
Saracens – Indian figs and Indian corn – Julius Caesar and
the Druids, Dante, Shakespeare – silkworms and
mulberries, rents and taxes, antediluvians, American
republics, astronomy and shell-fish . . .

Like the rushing of a torrent was the volubility of the
Conte Garrolo! Yet one failed to receive any distinct
impression from what he said – so unconnected and rapid
was the jumbling together of his subjects and eloquence!
Nevertheless, his liveliness diverted us to the utmost, the
more from its contrast to the lethargic and monotonous
conversation of most of our former hosts – and we
wondered if the Contessa would talk a tenth part as much,
or as loudly.

Supper was ready sooner than in most of these houses,
and when it was served, in came the Contessa, who was
presented to us by her husband with a crash of compliments
and apologies for her appearance, which put our good
breeding to the severest test. In all my life I never so heartily
longed to burst into merriment, for the poor lady, either
from ill-health or long habitual deference to her loquacious
spouse, said nothing to the world but, 'Nirr si' or 'Nirr no'
– which smallest efforts of intellecutal discourse she

continued to insert between the Count's sentences in the meekest way, like Pity between the drummings of despair in Collins' *Ode to the Passions*.

'Excuse her, excuse her,' thundered the voluble Conte, 'excuse her – supper, supper, supper – the table is ready, the table is ready –

'*Nirr si.*'

'Quick, quick, quick, quick.'

'*Nirr si, nirr no.*'

'Sit down, sit down – her sister died four months ago.'

'*Nirr si.*'

'Eat, eat!'

'*Nirr no.*'

'Macaroni? Chicken? – her mother is dead, she cries too much – Anchovies? Soups? Eggs?'

'*Nirr no.*'

'Signori strangers, take some wine. Countess, be merry!'

'*Nirr si.*'

& Etc, etc.

It was a most trying and never-ending monologue, barring the choral nirr si and no, and how it was we did not go off improperly into shrieks of laughter I cannot tell!

Instantly after supper the Contessa vanished, and the Conte bustled about like an armadillo in a cage, showing us our room, and bringing in a vast silver basin and jug and towels with the most surprising alacrity, and although the ludicrous greatly predominated in these scenes, yet so much prompt and kind attention was shown to the wants of two entire strangers by these worthy people was most pleasing.

The next day, the bustling Count whisked us all over the town, into the church, the castle, the lanes – showed us the views, the walls, the towns, the villages – manuscripts, stables, the two mules, and the purple velvet saddle and crimson housings, with coronets, and Garrolo, Garrolo, Garrolo, Garrolo – tutto-tutto-tutto – put us in charge of a peasant to show us a short cut to Adore – shook hands fifteen times with each of us, and then rushed away with a frantic speed: 'To write down some poetical thoughts; to give orders to the servants; to sell a horse; to buy some grain; to gather some flowers; to console the Countess. Goodbye! Goodbye!'

Addio, remarkable Conte Garrolo! a merry obliging little man you are as ever lived, and the funniest of created counts all over the world!

10 August 1847.

No Such A Thing As A Gooseberry

It was a very old palazzo in the town of Rocella, with tiny rooms, built against a rock, and standing on the extreme edge of the precipice towards the sea. The family received us cordially – Don Giuseppe, and Don Aristide, the Canonico, and Don Fernando – and during the doleful two hours preceeding supper, we sat alternately watching the stars, or listening to the owl-answering-owl melody in the rocks above our heads, or fought bravely through the *al solito* questions about Inghilterra, its produce, and the tunnel under the Thames.

I confess, though, to having been more than once fast asleep and, waking up abruptly, answered at random, in the vaguest manner, to the applied catechetical torture. I will not say what I did not aver to be the natural growth of England – camels, cochineal, sea-horses or gold-dust – and as for the *célèbre tunnel*, I fear I invested it drowsily with all kinds of fabulous qualities!

Supper was at last announced, and an addition to our party was made in the handsome wife of Don Ferdinando, and other females of the family – though I do not think they shared greatly in the conversation. Vegetables and fruit alone embellished the table. The world of Rocella particularly piques itself on the production and culture of fruit; and our assertion that we *had* fruit in England was received with thinly hidden incredulity.

'You confess you have no wine – no oranges – no olives – no figs?' said our host. 'How, then, *can* you have apples, pears or plums? It is a known fact that *no* fruit does or can

grow in England, only potatoes and nothing else whatever.
Why, then, do you tell us that which is not true?'

It was plain we were looked upon as vagabond imposters.

'But indeed we *have* fruit,' said we, humbly. 'And, what
is more, we have some fruits which you do not have at all!'

Suppressed laughter and supercilious sneers, when this
assertion was uttered, nettled our patriotic feelings.

'Oh, what fruit can you possibly have that we have not.
You are making fun of us! Name your fruits then – these
fabulous fruits!'

'We have Currants,' said we, 'many Currants – and
Gooseberries – and Greengages!'

'And what are Gooseberries and Greengages?' said the
whole party, in a rage, 'there are no such things – this is
nonsense!'

So we ate our supper in quiet, convinced almost that we
had been telling lies. That Gooseberries were unreal and
fictitious; Greengages a dream!

13 August 1847.

A BED OF MACARONI

Life at Stignano is oppressive. The famiglia Caristo would
never leave us alone. When they do not catechise, they stand
in a row and stare at us with all their might. And the
grandpaternal Caristo is a thoroughly scrutinising and
insatiable bore!

At dinner, also, there was a most confused assemblage of
large dogs under the tables who fought for casual crumbs
and bones, and when they did not accidentally bite one's
extremities, rushed, wildly barking, all about the little
room.

But the most remarkable accident during our stay was
caused by a small juvenile Caristo who, during the mid-day
meal, climbed abruptly on to the table and, before he could
be rescued, performed a series of struggles among the

dishes, which ended by the little pickle's losing his balance and collapsing into the very middle of the macaroni dish! The self-same dish from which we rejoiced to think we had previously helped ourselves!

One sees in Valentines: Cupids on beds of roses, or on birds' nests. But a slightly clothed Calabrese infant sitting in the midst of a hot dish of macaroni appears to me a perfectly novel idea!

14 August 1847.

THE WEARISOME OLD MAN OF VETERE

In the large dining room of the mansion were assembled many female and juvenile Asciutti, all very ugly. Hitherto we are not struck by Calabrian beauty in the higher orders, though many of the peasant girls are pretty.

The ladies spoke not during dinner, and the whole weight of the oral entertainment fell on the erudite grandfather, who harangued loftily from his place at the end of the table. It was Wednesday, and there was no meat, as is usual on that day in South Italian families.

'It would be better,' said the authoritative elder, 'if there were no such thing as meat – nobody ought to eat *any* meat. The Creator never intended meat, that is the flesh of quadrupeds, to be eaten. No good Christian ought to eat flesh – and why? The quadruped works for man while alive, and it is a shame to devour him when dead. The sheep gives wool, the ox ploughs, the cow gives milk, the goat cheese.'

'What do the hares do for us?' whispered one of the grandsons.

'Hold your tongue!' shouted the orator. 'But fish, what do *they* do for us? Does a mullet plough? Can a prawn give milk? Has a tunny any wool? No. Fish, and birds, also, were therefore created to be eaten!'

At this a silence fell and no sooner was dinner over, than

we made our intention of leaving known to the Asciutti family.

'Oh heavens! Oh rage! Oh what do I hear?' screamed the Nonno in a paroxysm of anger. 'What have I done that you will not stay? How can I bear such an insult! Since Calabria was Calabria, no such affront has ever been offered to a Calabrian! Go – *why* should you go?'

In vain we tried to assuage the grandsire's fury. We had stayed three days in Gerace, three in Reggio, two in Bova and Stilo, and not one in Vetere! The silent father looked mournful, the grandsons implored; but the wrathful old gentleman, having considerably endangered the furniture by kicks and thumps, finally rushed down stairs in a frenzy, greatly to our discomfiture.

What a wearisome old man was the Asciutti Nonno!

18 August 1847.

THE STORY OF BARON WHEREFORE?

In a spacious salon sat a party playing at cards, and one of them, a minute gentleman with a form more resembling that of a sphere than any person I ever remember to have seen, was pointed out to me as the Baron whom I sought. But excepting by a single glance at me, the assembled company did not appear aware of my entrance, nor, when I addressed the Baron by his name, did he break off the thread of his employment, otherwise than to say:

'One, two, three – yes, sir – four, five – your servant, sir – makes fifteen.'

'Has your Excellency received an introductory letter from the Cavalier de Nava?' said I.

'Five, six – yes, sir – make eleven,' said the Baron.

This, thought I, is highly mysterious.

'Can I and my travelling companion lodge in your house, Signor Baron, until tomorrow?'

'Three and six are nine,' pursued the Baron with renewed

attention to the game, 'Ma *perchè*, signore? Why, what for, Sir?'

'*Perchè*, there is no inn in this town; and, *perchè*, I have brought you a letter of introduction!' rejoined I.

'Ah, si, si, si, signore, pray favour me by remaining at my house – two and seven are nine – eight and eleven are nineteen.'

. And again the party went on with the Giuoco . . .

When the Baron joined us later, few words were said but those of half-suppressed curiosity as to where we came from. And the globose little Baron himself gradually confined his observations to the single interrogative, '*Perchè*?', which he used in a breathless manner, on the slightest possible provocation. Supper followed, every part of the entertainment arrayed with the greatest attention to plenty and comfort.

But the whole circle seemed ill at ease, and regarded our looks and movements with unabated watchfulness, as if we might explode, or escape through the ceiling at any unexpected moment; so that both hosts and guests seemed but too well pleased when we returned to our room, and the incessant, '*Perchè? perchè? perchè?* was, for the evening at least, silenced.

As usual, we rose before sunrise.

'O Dio! *Perche?*' said the diminutive Baron who was waiting outside the door, lest perhaps we might have attempted to pass through the keyhole. Endless interrogatories followed and more '*perchès*' than are imaginable.

'We want to make a drawing of your pretty little town,' explained I; and in spite of another perfect hurricane of '*perchès*', out we rushed, followed by the globular Baron, in the most lively state of alarm, down the streets, across the river on stepping stones, and up the opposite bank, from the steep cliffs of which, overhung with oak foliage, there is a beautiful view of Gioisa on its rock.

'I am going to draw for half-an-hour' said I.

'Ma – *perchè?*' said he.

It was evident that do or say what I would, some mystery

was connected with each action and word; so that, in spite
of the whimsical absurdity of the eternal 'what fors' and
'whys', it was painful to see that, although our good little
host strove to give scope to his hospitable nature, our stay
caused more anxiety than pleasure.

His curiosity, however, was to be tried still further; for,
having heard that Gioisa was famous for the manufacture of
sugarplums, we resolved to buy some; but when we asked
where the confection could be purchased the poor Baron
became half breathless with astonishment and suspense, and
could only utter over and over again:

'It is not possible! Oh, great heavens! Sugarplums! *Perchè*,
sugarplums?'

But sugarplums we were determined to have, and
forthwith got the direction to the confectioners, wither we
went and brought an immense quantity – the mystified
Baron following us to the shop and back, saying
continually:

'*Perchè, perchè* sugarplums? O *perchè*?'

We then made ready to start and, taking leave of the
Palazzo, the anxious Baron thrust his head from a window
and called out,

'But stop – *perchè* do you go? Stay to dinner! *Perchè* not?'
And still he went on, '*Perchè* drawings? *Perchè* sugarplums?'
till the last '*perchè*?' was lost in the distance as we passed
round a rock and crossed the River Romano.

Long did we indulge in merriment at the perturbation our
visit had occasioned to our host, whom we shall always
remember as 'Baron Wherefore?'

19 August 1847.

THE BROBDIGNAGIAN LANDLADY

When we reached Palmi we went to a locanda which had
been named to us by someone on the road – but in going
there, old Ciccio twice shook his head and said, 'No good –
dighi, doghi, da!', from which we did not augur any great

success in our search for rooms.

When we arrived at the bottom of the scala, or staircase, all the upper part of it was filled up by the most Brobdignagian of living landladies! Moreover, this enormous woman was peculiarly hideous and clad in the slightest and most extraordinary of simple costumes.

True, the thermometer was at the highest, and the lady might be suffering from the great heat – but the apparition of her dishabille and globe-like form was so remarkable that we paused at the threshold of so formidable a hostess. She had evidently been sacrificing earnestly to Bacchus, and was as unsteady on her feet as clamorous with her tongue.

'Let us try some other locanda,' said we to each other, and were turning away when the monster landlady shouted out.

'O, my sons, come in, *come in!*'

But she saw her invitation was making no impression.

'Go, then, to the black devil!' quoth she, accompanying her words with a yell, and an abrupt ejection of a large broom from her right hand down the staircase.

We fairly fled the place without further discussion, and followed the silent but grinning Ciccio to another locanda . . .

25 August 1847.

II

ALBANIA

(1848)

GIORGIO AND THE POLITE POSTMASTER

Of Giorgio, dragoman, cook, valet, interpreter and guide on all my travels, I have as yet nothing to complain. He is at

home in all kinds of tongues, speaking ten fluently, an accomplishment common to many of the travelling Oriental Greeks, for he is a Smyrniote by birth.

In countenance my attendant is somewhat like one of those strange faces, lion or griffin, which we see on door-knockers or urn-handles, and a grim twist of his under-jaw gives an idea that it would not be safe to try his temper too much.

In the morning he is diffuse, and dilates on past journeys. After noon, his remarks become short and sententious – not to say surly. Any appearance of indecision evidently moves him to anger speedily. It is necessary to watch the disposition of a servant on whom so much of one's personal comfort depends, and it is equally necessary to give as little trouble as possible, for a good dragoman has always enough to do without extra whims or worryings from his employer . . . !

To make sure of as long a day as possible in Greece, the elaborate northern meal of breakfast may be well omitted. A good basin of coffee and some toast is always enough, and is soon over, and until starting-time, there are always stray minutes for sketching.

The inhabitants of Yenidje are such imperturbable people that it is not easy to discover their thoughts. The outskirts of this quiet town are most peaceful and rural, and the picturesque odds and ends within might occupy the man of the pencil pleasantly and profitably.

While Giorgio and I are taking a parting cup of coffee with the postmaster, I unluckily set my foot on a handsome pipe bowl – pipe bowls are always snakes to near-sighted people as they are scattered in places quite remote from the smokers, who live at the farther end of prodigiously long pipe-sticks.

Crash! Over went the pipe-bowl – but nobody moved. The only response was an apologising – translated by Giorgio – from the polite Mohammedan who said:

'The breaking of such a pipe-bowl would indeed, under ordinary circumstances, be disagreeable. But in a friend every action has its charm!'

This speech immediately recalled the injunction of the Italian to his son on leaving home:

'Whenever anybody treads upon your foot in company and says, "I beg your pardon," – only reply: "On the contrary, you have done *me* a pleasure!"'

14 September 1848.

THE MAD DERVISH OF TYRANA

The immediate neighbourhood of Tyrana is delightful. Once outside the town you enjoy the most charming scenes of quiet among splendid planes and the clearest of streams.

The afternoon was fully occupied in drawing on the road from Elbassan, whence the view of the town is beautiful. The long line of peasants returning to their homes from the bazaar enabled me to sketch many of their dresses in passing. Of those whose faces were visible – for the great part wore muslim wrappers – some few were very pretty, but the greater number had toil and careworn faces.

I also saw a number of dervishes wearing high, white felt, steeple-crowned hats, with black shawls round them . . .

That night, no sooner had I retired to my pig-sty dormitory, and had put out my candle and was preparing to sleep, than the sound of a key turning in the lock of the next door to that of my garrett, disturbed me. And, lo! broad rays of light illuminated my detestable lodging from a large hole, a foot in diameter, besides two or three others, just above my bed. At the same time, a whirring, humming sound, followed by strange whizzing and mumblings, began to pervade the apartment!

Desirous to know what was going on, I crawled to the smallest chink, without encountering the rays from the great hiatus, and *what* did I see?

None other than one of the maniac dervishes I had seen that morning in the very next room! He was performing the most wonderful evolutions and gyrations: spinning round and round for his own private diversion! First on his legs, and then pivot-wise, *sur son séant*, and indulging in numerous other pious gymnastic feats.

Not quite easy at my vicinity to this very eccentric neighbour – and half anticipating a twitch from the brass-hooked stick he was waving about – I sat quite still waiting for the outcome of this performance, whatever it might be.

It was simple. The ancient buffoon pulled forth some grapes and ate them – after which he gradually relaxed in his twirlings and finally fell asleep!

28 September 1848.

THE TIK-TOK MAN

In the arabesqued and carved corridor, to which a broad staircase conducted me, were hosts of Albanian domestics. Upon my letter of introduction being sent into the Bey, I was almost instantly asked into his room of reception.

The room was a three-windowed, square chamber, where, in a corner on a raised divan sat Ali Bey of Kroia – a lad of eighteen or nineteen dressed in the usual blue frock-coat adopted by Turkish nobles or officers.

A file of kilted and armed retainers were soon ordered to

marshal me into a room where I was to sleep, and the little Bey seemed greatly pleased with the fun of doing hospitality to so novel a creature as a Frank!

My dormitory was a real Turkish chamber; and the raised cushions on three sides of it – the high, square, carved wooden ceiling – the partition screen of lofty woodwork, with long striped Brusa napkins thrown over it – the guns, horse-gear, etc., which covered the walls – the fire-place, closets, innumerable pigeon-holes, the green, orange and blue-stained glass windows – all appeared so much the more in the light of luxuries and splendours when found in so remote a place as Kroia!

It was not easy to shake off the attentions of ten full-dressed Albanian servants, who stood in much expectation, till, finding I was about to take off my shoes, they made a rush at me and showed such marks of disappointment at not being allowed to make themselves useful, that I was obliged to tell Giorgio to explain that we Franks were not used to assistance every moment of our lives, and that I should think it obliging of them if they would leave me in peace!

After changing my dress, the Bey sent to say that supper would be served in an hour – he having eaten at sunset – and in the meantime he would be glad of my society. So I took my place on the sofa by the little gentleman's side, and Giorgio, sitting on the ground, acted as interpreter.

At first, Ali Bey said little; but soon became immensely loquacious, asking numerous questions about Stamboul and a few about Franks in general – the different species of whom he was not very well informed upon. At length, when the conversation was flagging, he was moved to discourse about ships that went without sails, and coaches that were impelled without horses.

To please him, I drew a steamboat and a railway carriage. He asked if they made any noise – to which I replied by imitating both the inventions in question in the best manner I could think of – 'Tik-tok, tik-tok, tik-tok, tokka, tokka, tokka, tokka, tokka – tok (crescendo), and 'Squish-squash, squish-squash, squish-squash, thump-bump' – for the land and sea engines respectively.

It was a noisy novelty, which so intensely delighted Ali Bey that he fairly threw himself back on the divan, and laughed as I never saw a Turk laugh before! For my sins, this imitation became fearfully popular, and I had to repeat 'squish-squash' and 'tik-tok' till I was heartily tired.

The only recompense this wonderfully little Pasha offered me was the sight of a small German writing box (when new it might have cost three or four shillings) containing a lithograph of the singer Fanny Ellsler in the lid. This was brought in by a secretary attended by two militarymen and was evidently considered as something uncommonly interesting!

So when this very intellectual intercourse was over, I withdrew to my wooden room and was glad of a light supper before sleeping.

29 September 1848.

THE ANTICS OF MOOSTAFA THE IMP

Towards evening, the lines of purple Tomóhrit were exquisitely fine. Every wrinkle and chasm in its vast sides is perfectly delineated from the market-place of Berát (that is, in fact, at this season, the dry bed of the river, which does not rise so high until much later in the year!), the broad foreground of yellow sand, covered with a never-failing succession of resposing groups, was charming.

A great part of the people sit and smoke, by tens and twenties, after the indolent fashion of the Albanians. And the community seemed to enjoy keenly the pranks of a little imp whom they called Moostafa.

Long mounted lines of elderly men, on asses, were returning to Berát, from vineyards or village gardens higher up the river. And, as they passed by, Moostafa teased the old-men-bearing-quadrupeds to a fearful degree by pulling

their tails and avoiding – with will-o'-the-whisp activity –
all the blows aimed at him by the incensed riders!

At length, the furious victims dismounted – when,
behold, little Puck was running away like lightning. The
exasperated ancients, knowing all hope of chase to be out of
the question, remounted slowly and sullenly, to find their
graceless persecutor at their backs in two minutes, when the
same scenes occurred again, *da capo*!

All the crowd, of four or five hundred spectators, were
greatly interested in these gambols, and yelled with delight
at each of Moostafa's exploits – though they were nearly
ended by one kicking mule putting the little buffoon's head
in jeopardy!

15 October 1848.

THE SONG OF THE BO-BO MAN

I am desirous of seeing as much of the Khimáriote manners
and society as is possible, and so my host has asked two
gipsies to pass the evening with us, they being great
performers on the guitar which they accompany by singing.
And as it is not improbable we might have a dance also, he
has invited one of his own friends from Arghyro Kastro to
dine with us – a gentleman whose long, dishevelled hair fell
most dramatically over his shoulders and who, like the rest
of the 'society', rejoiced in bare feet and gaiters! In fact, my
arrival at Dukádhes seemed the signal for a sort of universal
soirée – and I was to promote the general hilarity by the gift
of an unlimited quantity of wine: an arrangement I willingly
acceded to for the sake of witnessing 'life in Khimara'.

In an hour or two came in the usual round tin table,
preceded by napkin and water, precursors of a good dish of
hashed mutton, and a plain roast fowl, which, with
tolerable wine, made no bad supper. After the repast is

done, a process of sweeping always goes on, a mere form,
but never neglected by these people. Unwilling to
incommode me, though, they swept most carefully all
around me!

Presently, the company came – and queer enough it was!
The two Messiers Zingari, or gipsies, are blacksmiths by
profession, and are clad in dark-coloured garments, once
white, now gray-brown. The contrast between them and
the Albanians round them, nearly all of whom have light
hair and florid complexions, is very striking.

The gipsy, all grin and sharpness, who plays second
fiddle, is continually bowing and ducking to me ere he
squats down. But the elder, or first performer, is absolutely
one of the most remarkable looking creatures I ever beheld!
His great black eyes peering below immensely thick arched
brows, have the most singular expression of cunning and
ferocity, and his black moustache and beard enclose a
mouth which, when shut, argues all sorts of tragic
obstinacies, but, on opening, discloses a grin of brilliant
ivory from ear to ear. Take him for all in all, anything so
like a diabolical South Sea idol I never yet saw living!

At first the entertainment was rather slow. The gipsies
had two guitars, but they only tinkled them with a
preparatory coquettishness, until another friend dropping in
with a third mandalino, a pleasing discord was by degrees
created that seemed to promise brilliant things for the
evening's festivities.

As the musical excitement increased, so did the audience
begin to keep time with their bodies, which this people,
even when squatted, move with the most curious flexibility.
An Albanian, sitting on the ground, goes plump down on
his knees, and then bending back, crosses his legs in a
manner wholly impracticable to us who sit on chairs from
infancy! While thus seated, he can turn his body half round
on each side as if on a pivot, the knees remaining
immovable.

Of all the gifted people in this way that I ever saw, the
gipsy guitarist was pre-eminently endowed with gyratory
powers – equal almost to the American owl, which, it is

said, continues to look round and round at the fowler as he circles about him, till his head twists off!

Presently, the fun grew fast and furious, and at length the father of the song – the hideous idol-gypsy – became animated in the grandest degree. He sang and shrieked the strangest minor airs with great skill, and energy enough to break it into bits. Everything he sang seemed to delight his audience, which at times was moved to shouts of laughter, at others almost to tears.

He bowed backwards and forwards till his head nearly touched the ground, and waved from side to side like a poplar in a gale. He screamed – he howled – he went through long recitatives, and spoke prose with inconceivable rapidity: and all the while his auditors bowed and rocked to and fro as if participating in every idea and expression.

I never saw a more decided instance of enthusiastic appreciation of song – if song it could be called, where the only melody was a wild repetition of a minor chorus: except at intervals when one or two of the Toskidhes' characteristic airs varied the musical treat!

The last performance I can remember having listened to, appeared to be received as a *capo d'opera*: each verse ended by spinning itself out into a chain of rapid little 'Bo's', ending in a chorus thus: 'Bo, bo-bo-bo, BO! – bo, bobobo, BO!'

Every verse was more loudly joined in than its predecessor. Until, at the conclusion of the last verse, when the unearthly idol-gipsy snatched off and waved his cap in the air – his shining head was closely shaved, except one glossy raven tress at least three feet in length! – the very rafters rang again to the frantic harmony:

'Bo, bo-bo-bo, bo-bo-bo, bo-bo-bo, bobobo, BO!' – the last 'BO!' uttered like a pistol shot and followed by a unanimous yell!

Fatigue is so good a preparation for rest, that after this savage mirth had gone on for two or three hours, I fell fast asleep and heard no more that night!

22 October 1848.

A Horrid Old Man Of Avlona!

Crossing a great water-course, our route lay at the foot of some hills, through ground more and more cultivated and cheerful, and about 1 p.m. we reached the village of Palasa. Here we halted, after a good morning's work, in a sort of piazza near a disreputable looking church, sadly out of repair.

A few Khimariotes were idling below the shady trees, and my guide, Anastasio, were soon surrounded and welcomed back to his native haunts, though I perceived that some bad news was communicated to him, as he changed colour during the recital of the intelligence and clasping his hands exclaimed aloud with every appearance of real sorrow.

The cause of this grief was, he presently informed me, the tidings of the death of one of his cousins at Vuno, his native place – a girl of eighteen whose extreme beauty and good qualities had made her a sort of queen of the village which, said Anastasio, I shall find a changed place, owing to her decease.

'I loved her,' said he, 'with all my heart, and had we been married, as we ought to have been, our lives might have been most thoroughly happy.'

Having said this much, and begging me to excuse his grief, he sat down with his head on his hand, in a mood of woe befitting such a bereavement.

Meanwhile, I reposed till the moment came for a fresh move onwards, when lo! with the quickness of light, the afflicted Anastasio arose and ran to a group of women advancing towards the olive trees. Among these, one seemed to interest him not a little.

As this woman drew nearer, I perceived that she was equally affected by the chance meeting. Finally, they sat down together and conversed with an earnestness which convinced me that the newcomer was a friend, at least – if not an actual sister – to the departed and lamented cousin of Vuno.

It was now time to start, and as the mules were loading, the Khimariote girl lingered, and I never saw a more exquisitely handsome face than hers: each feature was perfectly faultless in form. But the general expression of the countenance had a tinge of sternness, with somewhat traces of suffering. Her raven tresses fell loose over her beautiful shoulders and neck, and her form from head to foot was majestic and graceful to perfection. Her dress, too, the short, open Greek jacket or spencer, ornamented with red patterns, the many folded petticoat, and the scarlet, embroidered apron, admirably became her.

The girl was a perfect model of beauty, as she stood knitting, hardly bending beneath the burden she was carrying – her fine face half in shade from a snowy handkerchief thrown negligently over her head. She vanished when we were leaving Palasa, but reappeared below the village, and accompanied Anastasio for a mile or more through the surrounding olive groves, and leaving him at last with a bitter expression of melancholy which it was impossible not to sympathise with.

'Ah, Signore,' said Anastasio, 'she was to have been my wife, but now she is married to a horrid old man of Avlona, who hates her and she hates him, so they will be wretched all their lives.'

'*Corpo di Bacco*, Anastasio!' I exclaimed. '*Why*, you told me just now you were to be married to the girl who has just died at Vuno!'

'So I was, Signore; but her parents would not let me marry her, so I have not thought about her any more. Only now that she is dead I cannot help being very sorry. But Fortina, the girl who has just gone back, was the woman I loved better than anybody.

'Then why didn't you marry *her*?' said I.

'Because, because,' said the afflicted Anastasio, 'because I have a wife already, Signore, in Vuno, and a child six years old!'

23 October 1848.

III
CORSICA
(1868)

THE FAT WOMAN OF SARTENE

Sartene seems to be a populous place, with many large houses; but it was past sunset when I reached it, and I went at once to the Hotel d'Italie. For the Ajaccio diligence, which leaves Sartene at 6.30 p.m., had come thundering down the hill an hour before we arrived at the top of it, and, I suppose, to avoid any possibility of my being smuggled into any opposition locanda, the son of Madame Paolantonuccio, had come to meet me, and ensured my going to the right place by piloting me there himself! (Did I not, when I met that public conveyance, feel glad that I had not chosen to travel in it, knowing that the whole of the

beautiful scenery from here to Grosseto would have passed in the dark, seeing that the diligence only arrives at Cauro tomorrow morning at 7 a.m.)

At the hotel – as usual occupying only one floor of a house, in this instance a good sized one – I found several decent apartments untenanted, and was accompanied to the one I chose for myself by the landlady, a person of most astonishing fatness! Her face was nice and pleasant, but in figure she was like nothing so much as Falstaff disguised as the 'Fat Woman of Brentford.'

This bulky hostess looked on me with great favour, on finding that I was well acquainted with her native place, Como, and went into raptures when I talked about Varese and other Lombard localities. Nevertheless, at one moment I thought our acquaintance was to be of no long duration. For, having discovered me in the act of putting up my camp-bed – which at first, I believe, she thought was a photographic machine! – she suddenly became aware of its nature, called Giovanni and others of her household, and shouted out:

Ecc o un signore chi sdegna i letti di Corsica! – Here is a man who despises Corsican beds!'

And I do not know *what* might have followed this discovery, until my servant assured her that this was my

constant habit and by no means a reflection on her particular hotel! At this announcement, the amiable Fatima allowed herself to be pacified.

Later, the supper she provided was excellent, and she could not be satisfied without bringing far more dishes than were required, with fruits and smaller delicacies, such as olives, pickles, butter, etc., and the best of Tallano wine.

On my hostess asking me my opinion about various matters regarding Corsican inns, and on my gently suggesting that somewhat more cleanliness in the matter of floors, stairs, etc. (for, indeed, the state of these contrasts strangely with that of the very clean linen, table service, etc.), would be very likely to have beneficial effect on the recommendation of English visitors, Fatima spoke excitedly:

'*Como posso far tutto?* How can I do everything? In Corsica there are no servants; they consider service a dishonour and will starve sooner than work.'

Yet, she promised to do something for the unwashed floors.

'Can I,' she says, 'prevent those who come to my hotel, and through whom chiefly I am able to keep it up, from bringing their dogs, and throwing all the bones and bits of meat on the ground for them?'

Finally, she hit on an ingenious compromise.

'*So béne che vi dev'essere la pulizia, ma que in Sartene non é possible* – I know well that it is proper that things should be clean, but here in Sartene cleanliness is impossible.

'*Dunque, voglio colorire con color oscuro tutt' il fondo delle camere; cosi appunto non si scoprirà la sporcheri!* – Therefore I will colour with a dark tint the floors of all the rooms and so nobody will be able to see the dirt!'

20 April 1868.

THE MAN WHO SWALLOWED GENDARMES

At 5 a.m., Peter, my coachman, the trap and horses, folio, cloaks and provision for the day, are ready. Presently, M.

Quenza joining me, also with a full basket, we start for the mountains, soon leaving the main road and passing through an extensive cork forest, around which the soft, pleasant character of the Porto Vecchio scenery is very charming.

The cork woods are beautiful in colour, too, and in the texture of their thickly clustering foliage, and from their deep red stems where the bark has been removed. M. Quenza tells me he possesses 4,000 trees in this wood, each averaging a produce of ten sous annually.

Reaching the foot of the hills, at present covered with mist, we now begin to ascend towards the forest, and the road, one of the second class, called in Corsica, *Routes Forestières*, is henceforth carried, curving and winding with a steep ascent, up the face of the mountain; and though it is a good one, yet it has no parapet, and the fact of seeing mules pulling up a cart, the wheels of which are not more than an inch from the precipice's edge, by no means makes me more at ease in the carriage – and so I dismount and thenceforth walk!

My companion, the Maire, is full of cheery fun and stories innumerable. Presently, we pass a wild and singular looking individual tending two or three goats, who waves his hand to M. Quenza with an air of lordly patronage, quite unlike the respectful obeisance I observe paid to him by other peasants.

'But this poor fellow,' says M. Quenza, 'is a harmless lunatic, and his present delusion is that he is the King of Sardinia, which explains his magificent manner.'

A short time ago, apparently, the poor fellow was persuaded of a far less agreeable fact. He believed that he had swallowed two gendarmes!

The only remedy for this mishap was to eat nothing – in order to starve the intruders. Which resolution he rigidly adhered to, until his own life was nearly sacrificed.

When all but gone, however, he suddenly exclaimed, '*Ecco, tutti due son morti di fame!* – Now, both of them have died of hunger!' – and thereupon he resumed eating and work with joy!

24 April 1868.

THE MINISTER'S LAST RIDE

Shortly after noon I went on towards Bastelica, which is twenty kilometres distant from Cauro. Peter the oathful, who this morning has had some very bad fits of swearing and beating the horses, but who is at present in a comparatively placid mood, says, 'At these villages I am very often asked who you are, and I always say you are the *Ministro delle Finanze* – the Finance Minister of England.'

'But why,' said I, 'do you *say* such a thing?'

'Oh, partly because you wear spectacles, and have an air of extreme wisdom,' he replied, 'and partly because one must say *something* or other!'

A Minister of Finance seems to be grim Peter's beau idéal of earthly grandeur, and he has frequently spoken of having accompanied the illustrious M. Abbattucci, late Minister of Finance, to the country residence of that personage of Zicavo.

Now, as I was particularly in want of information concerning the road thither, I asked him one day: 'Did M. Abbattuci make the journey by Sta. Maria Zicchi, or by the village of Bicchisano?'

'He went by Grosseto to Sta. Maria,' was the reply.

'But,' said I, 'as the way from Ajaccio to Zicavo is long, where did the Minister stop? At Grosseto – or is there any other midway inn?'

'By no means,' said Peter, '*non di fermò punto, andava a giorno e notte* – he stopped nowhere, but travelled day and night.

'*Era mortissimo, ce Ministro delle Finanze, e non era che sue cenere chi si portava a Zicavo* – He was quite dead, that Minister of Finance, it was only his ashes that I took to Zicavo!'

3 May 1868.

THE VEXATIOUS MULE

Why does it seem a law established by destiny that the best points for making landscape drawings are so frequently in dangerous, uncomfortable, or filthy spots?

If your drawing is to be made in the country, *why* are you compelled to sit in a narrow and frequented mule-track, at the edge of a precipice, or below a crumbling rock, simply on account of the distance of a foot right or left preventing you seeing your subject owing to some intervening obstacle?

If in a town, *why* for a similar cause does the top of a wall, the centre of a thronged street, or the vicinity of an 'immondezzaio', become your inevitable seat?

And, oh painter, if you go to Corte ever beware of 'studying' below the houses thereof, lest the sudden opening of windows cause you eternal regret!

These reflections are prompted by the drawing I was making from a river bank, where my only possible position in order to see what I wanted, was on a narrow strip of ground between the torrent and a wall, and as every five minutes there came a vexatious mule along with a wide load of wood, I was often obliged, for fear of concussion, to mount the wall suddenly, while my man gathered up my folio and materials! Not an easy exercise for one of my globoscular form!

20 May 1868.

THE OWL WITH GLASS EYES

At dinner, the table of my host and hostess was without ceremony – but there was an exceedingly hearty welcome and very good cheer. Their little girl, Terese, an intelligent and darling child, was one of the party, and though not six years old, for good behaviour might have been twenty.

On my arrival, the great size of my spectacles had attracted the observant little lady, who had whispered to her mother, '*Comme il est charmant ce monsieur avec ses beaux yeux de verre?* – What a delightful gentleman with beautiful glass eyes!'

This was an admiration which was at least more gracious than that of a little girl at Chamouni some years back, who, after a long stare at me, exclaimed, '*Ah, que vos grandes lunettes vous donnet tout à fait l'air d'un gros hibou!* – How exactly your great spectacles make you look like a big owl!'

The evening passed in making drawings for little Terese, not unenlivened by snatches of merriment; for although I labour under the disadvantage of speaking French very ill, I nevertheless always find French acquaintances ready to help all deficiencies, and with the pleasant liveliness of their nature, to seize on any opportunity of my amusement.

My two French riddles delight my hosts. '*Quand est ce que vos souliers font vingt-cing?* – *Qand ils sont neuf et treize et trois (neufs et très étroits)*'; and '*Pourquoi dois tu cherir la chicorée?* – *Parceque c'est amere (ta mère)*'.

And, apropos to the appearance of potatoes at dinner, when the question is asked, '*On en mange beaucoup en Angleterre, n'est ce pas, monsier?*' they are charmed by my telling them the Irishman's saying:

'Only two things in this world are too serious to be jested about – potatoes and matrimony!'

21 May 1868.

There Was A Young Lady Of Ile Rousse, Who Wore A Rose In Her Tooth . . .

So I ramble through the town and on to the pier, beyond which there are works in progress connected with a small fort – for there is a little garrison at Ile Rousse – but finding no work to do, I go to the Hotel De Giovanni, to which the landlord at St. Florent had directed me.

The inn is large, and in an airy situation, and the rooms are clean, though not as much so as at the last place. As for the people, it is the same thing everywhere – simple in manner and thoroughly obliging; anxious to please the traveller, yet free from compliment and servility.

At 6.30 dinner was ready, served by a brisk damsel of no pretentions to beauty, but with a look of *espièglerie* and intelligence.

Yet, always she held a flower in her mouth! At the beginning of dinner it was a rose, latterly a pink!

She waited also at a table where seven or eight 'continentals' – *employés* – were dining. The dinner was good with some Balagna cherries and excellent cheese.

Later, when the damsel – who greatly resembled a lady on a Japanese teacup – brought some coffee, I said, 'May I venture to ask, without offence, why you continually carry a flower in your mouth?'

'And,' retorted the Japanese, 'may *I* venture to ask, without offence, why you, a stranger, inquire about matters which are not your affair, but mine?'

'*Perdoni*,' said I, 'do not be angry. I only had an idea that there might be a meaning in your doing so.'

Quoth she, '*Che cosa potrebbe mai signifcare*? – What could it possibly mean?'

'I thought,' said I, humbly, 'it might mean you were not to be spoken to. For how, with a flower in your mouth, could you answer?'

Whereat, the Corsican gravity gave way – and the hotel resounded with long peals of laughter from the Japanese!

29 May 1868.

FIVE

FOSS TAILS

or seventeen years Edward Lear's constant and much-loved companion was a striped tom cat called Foss – alternately referred to by his owner as 'Fofs' or 'Phos'. Apart from being featured in a good many of the artist's letters to his friends during the latter part of his life, the cat became familiar to the much wider audience of the general public when he was immortalised in Lear's famous poem, 'How Pleasant to Know Mr Lear' written in 1879. Verse five of this lively self-portrait declares:

> 'He has many friends, laymen and clerical,
> Old Foss is the name of his cat;
> His body is perfectly spherical,
> He weareth a runcible hat.'

Edward Lear had, in fact, been a cat-lover since his childhood, and some of his earliest sketches were of cats and kittens at play. Among his first professional drawings, too, were several of members of the cat family for John Gould's *Naturalists' Library* which appeared in the 1830s.

It was perhaps not surprising, therefore, that when forty years later, after years of travelling and staying in temporary accommodation and hotels, Lear finally settled in the first house of his own at San Remo in Italy, the Villa Emily, he should add a cat to the household of himself, his servant

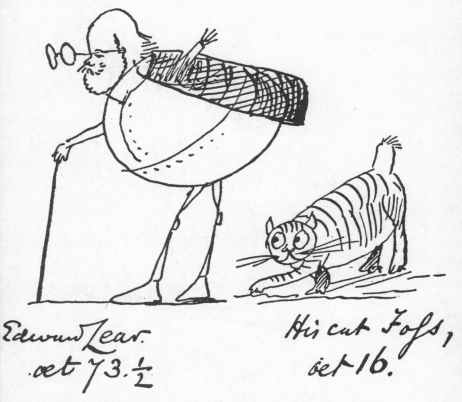

Edward Lear.
æt 73.½

His cat Foss,
æt 16.

Giorgio and a 'bandy-legged gardner' named Giuseppe. The cat he called Potiphar.

Unhappily, however, Potiphar did not settle, and disappeared one summer day never to be seen again. Lear, though, was determined that he *should* have a pet, and in November 1871 purchased a kitten named Foss. (The name was the middle syllable of a Greek word, and all the kittens from Foss's litter had been given the other syllables so that the complete family spelt out the entire word!)

Lear enthusiastically told his great friend, Chichester Fortescue, about the kitten in a typically amusing letter of 28 February 1872.

'I live very quietly,' he wrote. 'Sometimes I go to Church and sit under Mr. Fenton and hear all about the big fish as swallowed Jonah. A small walk daily – but this ain't a good place for walks. If you come I'll show you the Infant school,

PHOS.

and the Municipality, and Lemon valley, and an oil press, and a Railway station and a Sanctuary and several poodles – not to speak of my cat who has no end of a tail, because it has been cut off!'

This piece of surgery had been performed by Giorgio who believed in an old tradition that a cat would never wander from where it had left its tail! Lear has given us no indication as to how he regarded the operation – but certainly Foss' tail was lopped as all the later sketches show.

Foss did not immediately endear himself to his new master, however. For one morning a few days after his arrival he was discovered in Lear's study busy tearing the artist's letters and papers to shreds.

The kitten was promptly banished to Giorgio's kitchen, and Lear confided rather sadly in his diary that he thought this was

a 'pity'. He added, 'for he was a sort of companion – yet being very literally and really alone, it is perhaps as well to have no sham substitute for society.'

With the inherent mixture of cunning and affection which is the hallmark of the feline, Foss soon wormed his way back into Lear's affections and thereafter the two were inseparable, indoors and out.

Foss was soon inevitably to be seen scampering in Lear's footsteps as he walked around the gardens of the Villa Emily, or else waiting mischievously in the undergrowth to leap out at the artist when he passed by.

Lear also took to sharing his meals with Foss, handing out tit-bits of cold meat to the cat who lay purring by his side. His affection for the animal was even evidenced in a special nonsense menu he devised for some visitors who came to dine with him one evening. One of these guests fortunately retained this tribute to Foss which reads as follows:

Potage	Potage au Petit Puss.
Pour Poisson	Queues de chat, à la Aigùille.
First Entree	Orielles de Chat, frites à la Kilkenny.
	Pattes du Chat – aux chataignes.
Second Entree	Cotelletes de petit chat.
	(Sauce doigts de pied de Martyr – Tomata Sauce).
Rote	Gros Chat Noir.
Pour Legume	De Terre – sans pommes.
	Petite pierres curites à l'eau chaude.
Gibier	Croquet aux balles.
	Canards de Malta.
	Sauce au poivre, Sauce au sel.
Patisserie	Pátè de vers de soie sucre.
	Breadcrumbs à l'Oliver Cromwell (all of a crumble).
	Boudin de Milles Mouches.
	Compôt de Mouches Noires.

Lear not only found Foss irresistible as a companion, but at one stage he even believed he had artistic aspirations. In another letter to Chichester Fortescue in May 1882 he wrote:

'Foss the cat, having taken to sit from 5 to 8 a.m. under the cage of Giorgio's blackbird, since that very charming animal took to singing, we had very great hope of our cat's aesthetic tendencies, and had expected eventually to hear poor dear Foss warble effusively. But alas! it has been discovered that there is a hole in the lower part of Merlo's cage, and Foss' attention relates to pieces of biscuit falling through!'

This amusing scene may well have reminded Lear of a much earlier incident with a cat back in England in 1861 which he sketched in a little known item 'The Cat and the Hen' which is reprinted here. The text reads:

'Once upon a time a bird was ill, and a cat, bending down to it said, "How are you and what do you want? I will give you everything, only get well.' And the bird replied, 'If *you* go away, I shall not die!'''

Lear always made careful provision for Foss whenever his

work took him away from San Remo, and indeed he would
have liked to have been able to take him with him on his
travels, as a letter to Mr Fields, an American publisher who
had used a number of the artist's nonsense songs in his maga-
zine, *Young Folks*, indicates – albeit somewhat amusingly.
Discussing a project he had in mind to promote his nonsense
books, Lear wrote in October 1879:

'I have thought that I should stump all Europe and America
and wherever the English language is spoken, as the Writer of
the *Book of Nonsense*, with à view to collecting innumerable
sixpences so as to raise 7 or 8 Thousand Pounds to buy new
land and build another house! So look out for me and my cat

some fine day – by a Boston steamer on my way to San
Francisco!'

The reason for Lear being anxious to move house at this
time was because a hotel had been suddenly stuck up
immediately in front of his property, completely ruining his
view and his studio light. When, after considerable problems
and delay, he was finally able to secure a new piece of land and
build the Villa Tennyson (named after his friend, the famous
poet, Alfred, Lord Tennyson), Lear insisted that it be an exact
replica of the Villa Emily:

'Otherwise,' the artist told one of his correspondents, 'Foss
would *not* like it!'

The cat did, in fact make the transition to his new quarters
without any great problems and was as faithful a companion as

ever. Another letter from Lear to the wife of his local physician, Dr Hassall, dated 21 October 1885 again underlines the closeness between the man and his pet.

Lear writes, 'I did not say all I might have said to Dr.H about my health, thinking he might upbraid (or down-braid) me for doing more than I ought to do at my age, and considering how feeble I am, consequently – though I tell you in confidence – I did not tell him that I had climbed to the top of the tallest Eucalyptus tree in my garden and jumped thence into the Hotel Royal grounds – nor that I had leaped straight over the outer Villa Tennyson wall from the highroad – nor that I had run a race with my cat from here to Vintimiglia,

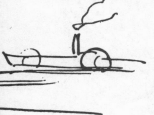

having beaten Foss by 8 feet and a half. Those facts you can impart to Dr.Hassall or knot as you like.'

At one juncture, Lear planned the ultimate tribute to his friend in the form of a series of intimate and comical sketches of the cat at work and play. Information about this scheme was given by author Angus Davidson in his first biography of the artist, *Edward Lear, Landscape Painter and Nonsense Poet*, published in 1938:

'Foss, Lear's constant companion for many years, achieved a celebrity denied to most cats, not only through the many allusions to him in Lear's letters, but through the series of lively but unflattering pictures of him in "The Heraldic Blazon of Foss the Cat" – "Foss Couchant", "Foss Rampant" etc.'

However, by the time he had done seven pictures Lear was

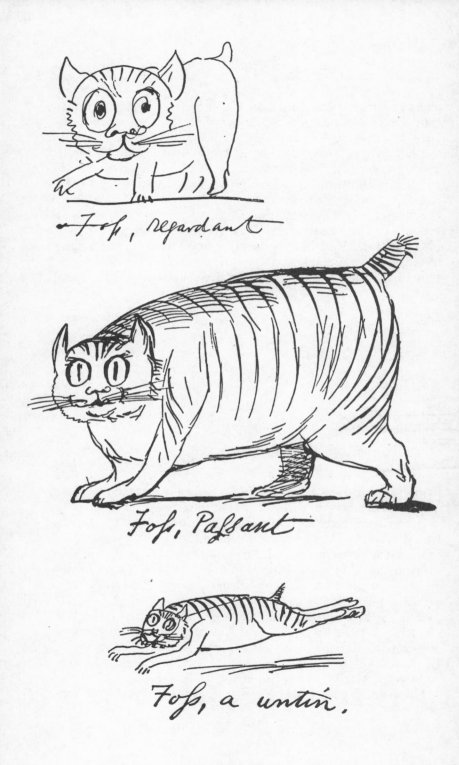

a Foss, regardant

Foss, Passant

Foss, a untin.

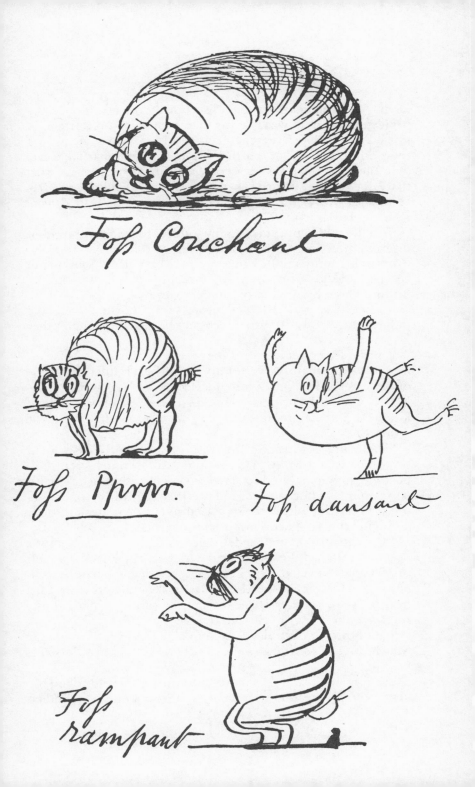

Foß Couchant

Foß Pprpr.

Foß dansait

Foß rampant

having misgivings about the idea. Finally, he abandoned the project, deciding it was 'a great shame to caricature a friend in this way'. The seven sketches have survived, however, and are reproduced here as yet another tribute to the remarkable cat.

In the light of all this evidence, it is not surprising to learn that Lear was devastated when Foss died in September 1887 – as another biographer, John Lehmann has written in *Edward Lear and His World* (1977):

'In a life which provided so few outlets for the great fund of intimate affection which Lear had always felt within him, the death of his companion, who appears as his faithful follower in so many of the self-caricaturing drawings of the last phase of his life, was a hard blow of fate.'

In fact, Foss's death even upset Lear's normally reliable judgement, as this letter to Chichester Fortescue of September 29 reveals:

'I must send you a line,' Lear wrote, 'and shall be glad to hear how you are now. As for my own life, it is full of sadness, of various grades: one of my oldest friends, Harvie Farquhar, Mrs.G.Clive's brother, has just died. He was always full of kindness and helpfulness for me, and his death is a great sadness.

'Then, my companion for thirty years – old Foss – died three days ago. I am so glad he did not suffer much, as he had become quite paralysed for two days. He had been my daily companion for thirty years, and was therefore thirty-one years old. I'm having a little tablet placed over where he is buried, and will send you a copy of it later on . . .'

Even the most casual reader will realise that this age cannot be correct. In fact, Foss had been with Lear since 1872 – a total of 17 years. Nevertheless, Lear compounded the error on the headstone he erected over Foss's last resting place below a fig tree in a shady corner of the orange walk in the Villa Tennyson's grounds. For it stated in Italian:

'Qui Sotto Sta Sepolto Il Buon GATTO FOSS Er in Cas Mia 30 Anni E Mori Il 26 Sept 1887 Di Eta 31 Anni – Edoardo Lear.'

Lear himself was not, of course, to survive his old friend for very long. His health had been declining for some years and he finally passed away quietly in the villa just over three months later. But both of them were destined to achieve immortality: Lear as a painter and even more so as the creator of nonsense prose, verse and songs; and Foss as the subject of some of his master's most delightful and informal sketches.

It is as a tribute to both of them in this centennial year that I have assembled in the pages of this book what is certainly the most widespread selection of Foss sketches to appear in a single volume.

I'm sure it is something that both would approve of, and as Lear himself might well have said in his own inimitable way:

> 'O pumpkins!
> O periwinkles
> O pobblesquattles!
> What a pussycat!'

Foss

SIX

PUFFLES OF PROSE

n December 1877 Lear published his fourth and last book of nonsense, *Laughable Lyrics*. (The earlier titles were, of course, *The Book of Nonsense*, 1846; *Nonsense Songs, Stories, Botany and Alphabets*, 1871; and *More Nonsense*, 1872.) He had been compiling material for this collection spasmodically during the previous five years in between working on a number of commissioned paintings and a series of watercolour drawings which he mass–produced for public sale and which, because of the demands they made on his failing strength and eyesight, he referred to somewhat grimly as his 'Tyrants'. *Laughable Lyrics* proved every bit as popular with the public as its predecessors had done, and contained several classic pieces of nonsense including 'The Pobble Who Has No Toes' and 'The Dong With The Luminous Nose.' Interestingly, Lear himself originally wanted to call this volume *Learical Lyrics and Puffles of Prose*, but was dissuaded by his publisher, Robert Bush, who then repaid him for his compliance by going bankrupt in June 1880, owing him a great deal of money! To complete this disaster, Bush had even lost all the printer's blocks for the three previous nonsense books.

Research into the manuscripts, diaries, journals and letters that survived Lear's death and were not destroyed by Frank Lushington, has subsquently brought to light more than enough items of nonsense to fill a fifth volume, perhaps even more. And so in the pages which follow I have brought

together some of the most amusing of these uncollected
pieces, which cannot be more aptly described than with Lear's
own words as 'Puffles of Prose.' Of particular interest, I
believe, are the short stories 'The Revenge of Pentedatilo' and
'The Land of the Blompopp Tree' which would grace any
anthology of fantasy tales. 'The Revenge of Pentedatilo' was
written by Lear during his tour of southern Italy in 1847 and is
based on a local legend which was related to him. It is a
memorable tale of Gothic horror. 'The Land of the Blompopp
Tree', on the other hand, is a humorous fantasy about a
journey to the Moon complete with a description of the inhabitants and the fauna to be found there. Lear wrote the story in
February 1882, and though much of it is unashamed – though
imaginative – 'nonsense', he was one of the earliest writers of
this kind of 'science fiction' to appreciate that a state of weight-
lessness exists on the Moon!

THE PAINTER AND THE TIPSY CLERK

I'm a landscape painter, and I desire you to like me as sich, or not at all. If I grow worse in my professional power, be sure I shall worsen in all ways.

I have a house full of books and a little bedroom and a small parlor and a big loft made into a study – which would be pleasant if the cats didn't bumble into it every five minutes!

All that costs five shillings a week – and I have three meals of food daily for one shilling and six pence. I'm finishing some water colour drawings by degrees and arranging in my mind some paintings for the winter.

There's only a curate as lives opposite and keeps bees. All the rest of the village is miners, which reside underground.

On Sundays I go to church where there is a congregation of seven or ten and a tipsy clerk.

O, beloved clerk! He reads the psalms enough to make you go into fits.

He said last Sunday, 'As white as an old salmon' (Instead of white as snow in Salmon.)

He also said, 'A lion to my mothers children' (for alien) and 'They are not guinea pigs' instead of guiltless!

O, how he pleases my foolish ears!

July 1851.

The aged & obese Landscape = painter will rejoice to come to H. Excellency tomorrow. ~

AN EGGZIBISSION AT
THE LORD HIGH BOSH-AND-NONSENSE
MAKER'S STUDIO

(Four ladies, having staid two hours, rise to go.)

First Lady: 'What a treat, my dear Mr. Lear! But how wrong it is of you to stay so much indoors! You should take more care of your health – work is all very well, but if your health fails you, you know you will not be able to work at all, and what could you do then? Now pray go out, and only see your friends before 12 or 1 in the morning.'

Second Lady: 'But how dreadful these interruptions must be! I cannot think how you ever do anything! *Why* do you allow people to break in on you so? It quite shocks me to think we have taken up so much time.'

Third Lady: 'Yes, indeed, these are the best hours of the day. You should never see anyone after 2 o'clock.'

Fourth Lady: 'You should work early, and then you could see your friends all the rest of the day. Interruptions must be so dreadful!'

(Enter four more ladies. The first four rush to them.)

All Eight Ladies: 'How charming! How fortunate! Dear Mary! Dear Jane! Dear Emily! Dear Sophia! Etc.'

Fifth Lady: 'How wrong of you dear Mr. Lear to be indoors this fine day!'

Sixth Lady: 'How you can *ever* work I *cannot* think! You

really should not admit visitors at all hours!'
Seventh Lady: 'But do let us only sit and look at these
beautiful sketches.'
Eighth Lady: 'O, how charming – and we will not go to
Lady O's.'
The Other Four Ladies: 'O, then we also will all sit down
again – it is so delightful!'
Chorus of Eight Ladies: 'What a charming life an artist's is!'
Artist: '---- D---n!'

April 1863.

No Such Person As Edward Lear

A few days ago in a railway as I went to my sister's, a
gentleman explained to two ladies – whose children had my
Book of Nonsense – that thousands of families were grateful
to the author (which in silence I agreed to) who was not
generally known – but was really Lord Derby!

Edward, Earl of Derby (said the gentleman) did not
choose to publish the book openly, but dedicated it as you
see to his relations – and if you transpose the letters LEAR
you will read simply EDWARD EARL!

Now there came into my mind at this moment a showing
forth which would clear up once and for all this statement
which had already appeared in several papers.

Says I, joining spontanious in the conversation, 'That is
quite a mistake! I have reason to know that Edward Lear the
painter and author wrote and illustrated the whole book.'

'And I,' says the Gentleman, says he, 'have good reason
to know, Sir, that you are wholly mistaken. *There is no such
a person* as Edward Lear.'

'But,' says I, 'there is – and I am the man and I wrote the
book!'

Whereon all the party burst out laughing and evidently
thought me mad or telling fibs. So I took off my hat and
showed it all round – with 'Edward Lear' and the address in

large letters. Also one of my cards and a marked
handkerchief!

At which amazement devoured those benighted
individuals and I left them to gnash their teeth in trouble
and tumult!

October 1866.

A Visit To The Zoo

I wen tup two the Zoological Gardings in Lunnon the other
day and drew a lot of Vulchers.

I saw the eagles and seagles and beagles and squeegles.
Leastwise, the big bears and all the other vegetables.

I also saw the little dragging, who is the Beast of the
Revialations, and here is his pikture.

November 1858.

A TUCKET TO RIDE

Scene: A railway station in the north of Scotland.
Persons: An old Scotchwoman and a railway clerk.

Old Woman: 'A Tucket.'
Railway Clerk: 'Whar till?'
O.W. (with more emphasis): 'A *Tucket*!'
R.C. (louder): 'Whar till?'
O.W. (fiercely): A *Tucket*, I say!'
R.C. (angrily): 'Whar till then?'
O.W.: 'You are a nasty speering body! What is't to you whar I am ganging to?'
At this the train draws up and a party of the old woman's friends call out: 'Jeanie! Jeanie! You'll be too late – have you na got your tucket?'
O.W.: 'Na! and I winna tell the old fellow whar I am going! What is it to him!'
The train goes on . . .

September 1860.

THE DREWNDID BOY

A Domestic Drama of Devonshire

Enter MARY
'Mary, has the boy come back from the Post with the letters yet?'
'Noa zur, hiss be drewndid!'
'He's what, Mary?'
'Hiss be drewndid zur in the pewerfil rain.'
'Well, it certainly does rain, Mary, but I hope he ain't drowned for all that.'
Exit MARY

Re-enter MARY
  'Here be tew litters, zur – the boy is all queet drewndid zur as ever you see!'

July 1851.

A RELIGIOUS OLD LADY OF SUSSEX

A rural old Lady I once knew in Sussex used to catechise her rustic maidservants on religious subjects.
  'What is Baptism?' she asked one girl.
  'Washing day, ma'am, if it comes once a week,' was the reply.
  'Good God! What an answer!' the old lady retorted. 'Tell me – do you know what is the Holy Sacrament?'
  'O, yes, Ma'am, very well,' came the bright response. 'Two biled iggs with vater-cresses!'

October 1882.

VIVA THE DIFFERENCE!

Have you heard the story of Emily F--- (or was it Miss G?) or some such female shrieker lecturing on the equality of the sexes? Apparently, she said, 'The sexes are intrinsically equal in spite of some little differences.'
  Whereupon there arose a roar from among her audience, 'Hurrah! for their little differences!'
  And after vain efforts to speak again, the shouters of 'Viva the little differences!' finally won the day – and the Lady Lecturer collapsed!

January 1884.

THE INEBRIATE MINISTER

It is recorded of a Scottish minister that he adapted his form of grace to what he thought the probable conditions of any banquet he attended.

Seeing only beer glasses on the table he would recite tersely, 'Bless the food of these puir miserable creatures!'

But, on the contrary, if champagne glasses were visible, he would begin in a loud and joyful tone, saying: 'Bountifully shower down all Thy blessings on these thy excellent servants!'

March 1870.

THE IRISH ARE A FUNNY PEOPLE

—148—

The Irish are funny people and the moment I meet one it is evident that England and Ireland are very different countries in many respects.

Among other odd ways of speech the common people never by any chance say, 'Yes, or 'No' – e.g. 'Is it time to go?' 'It is not, Sir.' or 'It is, Sir.'

'Have you cleaned my boots?' – 'I have, Sir.' or 'I have not, Sir.'

When we asked at Dublin if the Scientific Association meeting was over, they said, 'Indeed, and it isn't, but the strength of it is pretty well broken,' as if it were a revolution!

But one of the best absurdities is told of an old woman, who, though pretty well off, grumbled horribly. And when they said to her that for good clothes, prosperous children, a kind husband and comfortable home, she ought to thank God, said she:

'And sure don't he take it out of me in my Corns!'

September 1857.

A MATTER OF TIME

I once said to my servant, Giorgio, 'Why is there a ten minute difference between my watch and the hall clock? Which is wrong of the two – is my watch ten minutes too slow or the clock ten minutes too fast?'

'Your watch is all right, Sir,' he said grimly, 'because he is very warm in your pocket. Clock stand out in the cold hall and he go faster to warm himself.'

January 1868.

THE MAN WHO SHOT A CHERUBIM

Have you heard any of the stories of Vernon Fibber?
My friend Lady Hatherton once told me this man

declared he had seen two Cherubims on Mount Ararat. He fired at them with his gun.

One of the Cherubims flew away with a buzzing sound and an inestimable perfume. The other was wounded in the wing and fell to the ground.

The sportsman then took the creature home – so the Fibber's story goes – and kept him alive for six weeks on milk and eggs. But just as the Cherubim was getting strong a cat seized him and ate him up!

May 1875.

DINING ON ELEPHANT'S LEG

For a long time I fed on an immense leg of mutton – far, far larger than any leg of mutton I ever saw before or since.

But one day I remembered that I had gone to the window to see a Circus Company go by, and attached to that there was an elephant. And I then had the horrid recollection that the Circus had long since returned (I saw it pass by) but the elephant *never had*!

From that moment I felt what that large leg of preposterous mutton really was, '*e non mangiar avante*' – and I did not eat any more!

On the whole I do not recommend dead elephant as daily food!

September 1859.

FISH HURLING

Reading *The Times* one morning at breakfast in an Italian hotel, I suddenly came across news of the appointment of a friend to high office. Being of a demonstrative nature in matters that give me pleasure, I threw the paper up into the air and jumped aloft myself – ending by taking a small fried whiting out of the plate before me and waving it around my foolish head triumphantly till the tail came off and the body and head flew bounce over to the other side of the table d'hôte room.

Then only did I perceive that I was not alone, but that a party was at breakfast in the recess. Happily for me they were not English, and when I made an apology saying I had seen some good news of a friend of mine, these amiable Italians said:

'Hurrah, Signore, we are also delighted! If we had only got some little fish, too, we would throw them all about the room in sympathy with you!'

November 1865.

THE PACING POODLES

The night sea voyage, though far from pleasant, need not be as bad as might be anticipated. He is fortunate, who, after ten hours of sea passage can reckon up no worse memories than those of a passive condition of suffering – of that dislocation of mind and body, or inability to think straight-forward, so to speak, when the outer man is twisted, and rolled, and jerked, and the movements of thought seem more or less to correspond with those of the body. Wearily go by, 'The slow, sad hours that bring us all things ill,' and vain is the effort to enliven them as every fresh lurch of the vessel tangles practical or pictorial suggestions with untimely scraps of poetry, indistinct regrets and predictions,

couplets for a new *Book of Nonsense* and all kinds of inconsequential imbecilities – after this sort:

Had I not said, scores of times, such and such a voyage was the last I would make?

Tomorrow when 'morn broadens on the borders of the dark,' shall I see Corsica's 'snowy mountain tops fringing the (Eastern) sky?'

Did the sentinels of lordly Volaterra see, as Lord Macaulay says they did, 'Sardinia's snowy mountain-tops,' and not rather these same Corsican tops, 'fringing the southern sky?'

Did they see any tops at all, or if any, which tops?

Will the daybreak ever happen?

Will two o'clock ever arrive?

Will the two poodles above stairs ever cease to run about the deck?

Is it not disagreeable to look forward to two or three months of travelling quite alone?

Does it not, as years advance, become clearer that it is very odious to be alone?

Have not many very distinguished persons, OEnone among others, arrived at this conclusion?

Did she not say, with evident pleasure:

> 'And from that time to this I am alone,
> And shall be alone until I die'?

Will those poodles *ever* cease from trotting up and down the deck?

Is it not unpleasant, at fifty-six years of age, to feel that it is increasingly probable that a man can never hope to be otherwise than alone, never, no, never more?

Did not Edgar Poe's raven distinctly say, 'Nevermore?'

Will those poodles *be quiet*? 'Quoth the raven, nevermore.'
Will there be anything worth seeing in Corsica?
Is there any romance left in that island?
Is there any sublimity or beauty in its scenery?
Have I taken too much baggages?
Have I not rather taken too little?
Am I not an idiot for coming at all?
Are there not Banditti?
Had there not been Vendetta?
Were there not Corsican brothers?
Should I not carry clothes for all sorts of weather?
Must THOU not have taken a dress coat?
Had HE not many letters of introduction?
Might WE not have taken extra pairs of spectacles?
Could YOU not have provided numerous walking boots?
Should THEY have not forgotten boxes of quinine pills?
Shall WE possess flea-powder?
Could YOU not procure copper money?
May THEY not find cream cheeses?
Should there not be innumerable moufflons?
Ought not the cabin lamps and glasses to cease jingling?
Might *not* those poodles stop worrying?

Thus and thus, till by reason of long hours of monotonous rolling and shaking, a sort of comatose insensibility, miscalled sleep, takes the place of all thought, and so the night passes . . .

8 April 1868.

THE GERMAN PESSIMIST

An encounter on board a ship
bound for Bombay

German Pessimist: 'You vear spegtacles alvays?'
Edward Lear: 'Yes.'

G.P. 'They vill all grack in India. Von pair no use.'

E.L. 'But I have many pairs.'

G.P. 'How many?'

E.L. 'Twenty or thirty.'

G.P. 'No good. They vill all grack. You should have got of silver.'

E.L. 'But I have several of silver.'

G.P. 'Dat is no use. They vill rust. You might got gold.'

E.L. 'But I have some of gold.'

G.P. 'Dat is more vorse. Gold is alvays stealing!'

October 1872.

A RIDE ON A PHOCA

I keep a Phoca in my great cistern, whence it can easily out-be-got by the lower water course. I feed him four biscuits and a small cup of coffee in the early dawning.

One morning I thought I would go out to sea on his back – which I did more than half way to Corsica, for he swims orfle quick.

I had previously telegraphed to my friend Miss Campbell at Ajaccio, and she met me half way on her Porpoise – for she hasn't got a Phoca.

But our meeting was very short, owing to the amazing number of seagulls she had brought with her, who made such a d---d row that all conversation was unpossible!

December 1885.

THE LADY AND THE ORANGE

An English lady was 'doing' the sights of Corfu, and among others the churches. In the Greek cathedral, a beggar woman came and importuned the glittering Marchioness, who at that moment was indulging in the natural and pleasant act of sucking an orange.

This lady, after a time, paused and said – or implied – 'Silver and gold have I none', but such as she had, the half-sucked orange, she politely gave to the beggar woman.

But oranges being any number for half a penny on the island, the woman threw the fruit in her Ladyship's face and rushed frantically out of the desecrated edifice!

January 1858.

THE EAR TRUMPET

A very deaf lady who used an ear trumpet was dining with some friends in India. During a break between courses, the lady was asked a question by her next neighbour and after thrusting the ear trumpet up alongside her head replied, 'Yes.'

At that very moment, a native servant, approaching the two diners from behind, held out a bottle and enquired, 'Ice champagne, Mem?'

And concluding, consequently, that the 'Yes' he heard was in reply to his own question and mistaking the ear trumpet held up in front of him for a sort of glass – instantly poured into it and the lady's ear a deluge of the iced champagne!

The distraught lady immediately threw the ear trumpet and all onto her neighbour's satin waistcoast and a vast confusion ensued!

July 1874.

MY QUEEREST CHRISTMAS DAY

I was in Cochin which has many very pretty bits but is as flat as 50,000 pancakes. The fact it was Christmas Day meant that all the shops were closed.

After a walk, Giorgio and I returned to our hotel and awaited dinner. After a while we got some tin beef tea soup, and that, thank goodness, was good, though there had been a frightful dispute between the butler and the cook as to the mode of making it.

Following that came a leg of mutton, but absolutely *raw* – whereupon there was a burst of anger from the butler about the 'bad cook.' The mutton was sent away and Giorgio and I sat calmly talking of Christmas Days we had spent in the past.

Then the mutton came back – but it was wholly uneatable having been utterly smoked. The potatoes were also cold and hard. Lastly, a baked rice pudding which was just about edible.

Finally, the butler rushed in and declared wildly, 'Wicked him cook, he drinksy, drunksy! He go off with keys of cooky rook and forky room. Go tell principality, but now too late!'

It appeared to me that the butler *might* be right, but I couldn't understand him. Certainly, the queerest Xmas Day I have passed in years!

25 December 1874.

THE PECULIARITIES OF BEDS

There is little wisdom in trying new beds if you can avoid doing so. Even if they are perfectly clean, each one has its peculiarities, arising from some springs or wires of its inner constitution which can lead it to make noises of the most surprising and unexpected kinds!

It is impossible to prepare the mind sufficiently for the sudden sounds which occur even on moving your head in some of these beds – far more so when it is a question of 'turning round'.

At one place I rested, a spring in the mattress was loose, and at times it made a most remarkable *humming*! While in another instance, lengthy and mouse-like *squeakiness* came from some incoherence of the irons – as the invalid says in Wilkie Collins' *Woman in White*, 'Take it away, something about it creaks, *take it away*!'

Therefore, henceforth, wherever I go I shall not forsake my old camp folding-bed!

May 1868.

THE FABLE OF THE HORN-RIMMED
SPECTACLES

Once upon a time, three poor students, all very near-sighted, and each possessing a single pair of horn-rimmed spectacles, set out to walk to a remote university, for the purpose of competing for a Professorship.

On the way, while sleeping by the road side, a thief stole their three pairs of horn-rimmed spectacles.

Waking, their distress was great: they stumbled, they fell, they lost their way; and night was at hand, when they met a pedlar.

'Have you any spectacles?' said the three miserable students.

'Yes,' said the pedlar, 'exactly three pairs; but they are set in gold, and with magnificent workmanship; in fact, they were made for the King, and they cost so much – '

'Such a sum,' said the students, 'is absurd; it is nearly as much as we possess.'

'I cannot,' the pedlar replied, 'take less; but here is an ivory-handled frying-pan which I can let you have for a trifling sum, and I strongly recommend you to buy it because it is such an astonishing bargain, and you may never again chance to meet with a similarly joyful opportunity.'

Said the eldest of the three students, 'I will grope my way on as I can. It is ridiculous to buy a pair of this man's spectacles at such a price.'

'And I,' said the second, 'am determined to purchase the ivory-handled frying-pan; it costs little, and will be very useful, and I may never again have such an extraordinary bargain.'

But the youngest of the three, undisturbed by the laughter of the two others, bought the gold-rimmed spectacles, and was soon out of sight.

Thereon, number one set off slowly, but, falling into a ditch by reason of his blindness, broke his leg, and was carried back, by a charitable passer-by in a cart, to his native town.

Number two wandered on, but lost his way inextricably, and, after much suffering, was obliged to sell his ivory-handled frying-pan at a great loss, to enable him to return home.

Number three reached the university, gained the prize,

and was made Professor of Grumphiology, with a house and fixed salary, and lived happily ever after.

    Moral – To pay much for what is most useful, is wiser than to pay little for what is not!

11 April 1868.

THE REVENGE OF PENTEDATILO

A Gothic Tale

For centuries, the families of the two feudal possessors of the towns of Pentedatilo and Montebello in the Kingdom of Naples had been deadly foes, and they ruled, or fought for, the adjoining country from their strongholds in persevering enmity.

    The Baron of Montebello, a daring and ferocious youth, was left heir in early life to his ancestral estates and rights, and fell in love with the only daughter of the Marchese Pentedatilo. But, although the young lady had contrived to acquaint her lover that her heart was his, her hand was steadfastly denied him by the Marchese, whom the memory of long injuries and wars hardened in his refusal.

    Opposition, however, did but increase the attachement of the young lady, and she at length consented to leave her

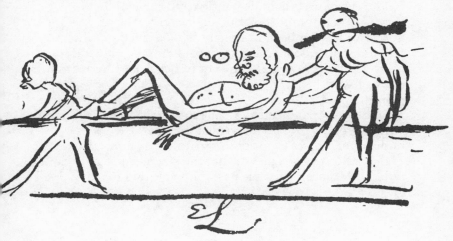

father's house and go with her lover. An arrangement was therefore made that on a certain night she would open a door in the otherwise impenetrable rock-fortress of Pentedatilo, and admit young Montebello with a sufficient force of his retainers to ensure the success of her elopement.

The Baron accordingly entered the castle, but finding that equal opportunity was presented him for vengeance on his feudal enemy – and for possesing himself of the object of his attachment – he resolved to make the most of both.

The young man went first to the chamber of the Marchese of Pentedatilo and found him sleeping by the side of the Marchesa, with a dagger at his pillow's head. The Marchese he then stabbed – yet not so fatally as to prevent his enemy placing his left hand on the wound, and with his right seizing his stiletto and plunging it into the heart of the innocent Marchesa, suspecting her as the author of death!

The Baron Montebello repeating his blows, the Marchese fell forward on the wall and his five blood-stained fingers left traces – still shown – on part of the ruined hall: a horrible memorial of the crime, strangely coincident with that of the form and name of the rock.

Immediately on the consummation of this double tragedy, the active young Baron Montebello carried off the young lady; his retainers also putting all the family of the Marchese to death.

All, that is, except one infant grandchild, whom a nurse saved by concealing in a crevice of the rocks . . .

The castle was then dismantled and the lady became the Baroness of Montebello. But she never spoke again – the horror of having been indirectly the destruction of her whole race occasioned her to become insane, and she poisoned herself within a month of her departure from her native town.

In the process of time, the child saved by the nurse grew up and was introduced as a page into the Montebello family – the Baron having re-married and being now the undisputed possessor of both territories as far as the sea.

But, after many years of life, the wretched man became wild with remorse for his past iniquities and made over all his possessions to the Church – provided only that no living descendant of the Pentedatili could be found.

This was seen as a decent proviso, apparently made without risk. But then, lo! the nurse and a small number of the old Marchese's friends proved, beyond any doubt, that the page was heir to the estates and the revenge of his ancestors!

And here you might suppose the story ended. But not at all.

The Baron's hatred returned on finding there was really something on which to exercise it – and he ordered the torture and execution of young Pentedatilo forthwith.

But now the tables were turned. The Baron's long reign of wickedness lent weapons to his adversary's cause, and, in his turn, the last scion of the murdered Marchese became a tyrant.

Forthwith the whole family of the Baron Montebello were destroyed before their parents' eyes, and the Baron himself was then blinded by order of his avenger, and chained for the rest of his days in the very room in which he had slain the grandsire Pentedatilo.

Finally, as if it were ordered that the actors in such a wholesale domestic tragedy were unfit to remain on Earth, the castle of Pentedatilo fell by the shock of an earthquake, crushing together the Baron and Marchese, with the nurse and every other agent in this Calabrian horror!

THE LAND OF THE
BLOMPOPP TREE

A Fantasy Story

I lately went one night to the Moon, returning next morning on a Moonbeam. Nothing is easier in that wonderful country than to travel thousands of miles in a minute.

These journeys are all done by means of Moonbeams,

which far from being mere portions of light, are in reality living creatures, endowed with considerable sogassity, and a long nose like the trunk of Nelliphant – though this is quite imperceptible to the naked eye!

You have only to whisper to the Moonbeam what you wish to see, and you are there in a moment – and it's nose or trunk being placed round your body, you cannot by any possibility fall.

The first thing you see are the Jizzdoddle Rocks, with two of the very remarkable planets which surround the Moon – rising or riz in the distance. These orange coloured and pea green orbs leave a profound impression of sensational surprise on the mind of the speckletator who first beholds them.

The second view is the Rumby-tumby Ravine, with the crimson planet Buzz and its five Satanites on the horizon. Here grow the Blompopp Trees, so called from the Blompopp, a gigantic and gorgeous bird which builds on its summit.

Also to be seen are the tall Vizzikilly Trees, the most common vegetation of the Lunar hemisphere. These trees grow to an immense height, and bloom only once in 15 years, when they produce a large crop of immemorial soapbubbles, submarine suckingpigs, songs of sunrise and silver sixpences – which last are ground into powder by the Lunar population, and drunk in warm water without any sugar.

So little is known of the inhabitants of the Moon, that a few descriptive but accurate notes relating to them may be of interest.

They do not in the least resemble the people of our world – as for instance they are all much broader than they are high. They have no hair on their heads – but on the contrary a beautiful crest of yellow feathers which they can raise or depress at will, like that of an ordinary Cockatoo.

From the tip of their nose, depends an elegant and affecting bunch of hair, sometimes extending to as much as 20 miles in length! It is considered sacreligious to cut it, being gradually wound round a silver-gilt post firmly placed in the ground, but removable at pleasure.

The faces of the more educated classes have a positively perverse and placid expression – not unlike the countenance of an oyster, while frequently a delicately doubleminded semi-visual obliquity adds a pathos to their pungent physiognomy.

These remarkable people, so unlike us, pass 18 months of their year (which consists of 22) in the strictest seclusion: suspended with their heads downwards, and tied carefully in crimson silk bags which are severely and suddenly shaken from time to time to select servants.

Thus, exempt from the futile and fluctuating fatuity of fashion, these estimable creatures pass an indigenous life of indefinite duration surrounded by their admiring ancestors, and despised by their incipient posterity.

The servants are not natives of the Moon, but are brought at great expense from a negative although nutritious star at a great distance, and are wholly of a different species from the Lunar population, having eight arms and eight legs each, but no head whatever – only a chin in the middle of which are their eyes!

The mouths of these servants (of which each individual possesses eight) being one in each little toe, and with these they discourse with an overpowering volubility and with an indiscriminatory alacrity surprising to contemplate. The conduct of these singular domestics is usually virtuous and voluminous, and their general aspic highly mucilangenous and meritorious.

Unfortunately, I have no further time at present to dilate further on other particulars of Lunar Natural History. The prevalence of two sorts of Gales: gales of wind and Nightingales. The general inebriety of the Atmosphere. Or even the devotional functions of the inhabitants, consisting chiefly in the immense consumption of Ambleboff pies . . .

February 1882.

LEARICAL LYRICS

A Selection of Uncollected
Riddles, Poems and
Nonsense Verses

RIDDLES

What nation talks the greatest nonsense?
The Boshmen!

★ ★ ★

What is the difference between a hen and a kitchen maid?
One is a domestic fowl, and the other a foul domestic!

★ ★ ★

Why couldn't Eve have the measles?
Because she'd *Adam* (had 'em).

★ ★ ★

When may the Lanes and Roads have shed tears of
sympathy?
When the street'*swept!*

★ ★ ★

Why need you not starve in the desert?
Because you can eat all the *Sand which* is there!

★ ★ ★

Why are the Sandwiches there?
Because there the family of *ham* was bread and mustard!

★ ★ ★

Is life worth living?
That depends on the Liver!

★ ★ ★

What letter confounds the Comets and Cookery?
G – for it turns Astronomy into Gastronomy!

★ ★ ★

What would Neptune say if they deprived him of the sea?
'I haven't a *n/otion!*'

★ ★ ★

Why are the kisses of mermaids pleasant at breakfast?
Because they are a kind of *Water Caresses*!

★ ★ ★

What Saint should be the Patron of Malta?
Saint Sea-bastian!

★ ★ ★

If a bee alights upon your nose why should you address it in
the imploring accent of a distracted lover?
Oh! Bee! Leave me! (Oh, believe me.)

★ ★ ★

Why are beginners on a Pianoforte like parasites on the
  backs of deceased fishes?
Because they are always running up and down their damned
  miserable scales!

★ ★ ★

What's the difference between the Czar of Russia and *The
  Times* newspaper?
One is the type of Despotism: the other despotism of Type!

★ ★ ★

Why should the Ilbert Bill be called the Filbert Bill?
Because many people think it hard to crack and unpleasant
  to swallow!
(*Editor's Note:* The Ilbert Bill, introduced to Parliament in
December 1883, was intended to make it legal for
Europeans in India to be tried by Indian judges.)

★ ★ ★

Where are the greatest number of Pawnbroker's shops?
Among the Pawnee Indians!

★ ★ ★

What is the answer to this riddle:
  Upon this Earth she walked
  Upon this Earth she talked
  Rebuking man of sin;
  Sinless she was no doubt
  And yet, from Heaven shut out
  She never will get in!
(The solution: Balaam's she-ass!)

★ ★ ★

POEMS

THE CHILDREN OF THE OWL AND THE PUSSY-CAT

Our mother was the Pussy-Cat, our father was the Owl,
And so we're partly little beasts and partly little fowl.
The brothers of our family have feathers and they hoot,
While all the sisters dress in fur and have long tails to boot.
  We all believe that little mice,
  For food are singularly nice.

Our mother died long years ago, she was a lovely cat,
Her tail was five feet long and grey with stripes, but what
  of that?
In Sila Forest on the East of far Calabria's shore
She tumbled from a lofty tree – none ever saw her more.

Our owly father long was ill from sorrow and surprise,
But with the feathers of his tail he wiped his weeping eyes.
And in the hollow of a tree in Sila's inmost maze
We made a happy home and there we pass our days.

From Reggian Cosenza, many owls about us flit
And bring us wordly news for which we do not care a bit.
We watch the sun each morning rise, beyond Tarento's
    strait,
We go out pleasure seeking, before it gets too late.
And when the evening shades begin to lengthen from the
    trees,
You'll find us merrily dancing as sure as bees is bees.

We wander up and down the shore,
Or tumble over head and heels, but never, never more,
Can see the far Gromboolian plains;
Or weep as we could once have wept o'er many a vanished
    scene:
This the way our father moans – he is so very green.

Our father still preserves his voice, and when he sees a star
He often sings to the strings of that original guitar.
The pot in which our parents took the honey in their boat,
But all the money has been spent, besides the £5 note.
The owls who come and bring us news are often sent away
Because we take no interest in the Politix of the day!

An unfinished fragment written in the summer of 1884.

ODE TO A CHINAMAN

Who art thou – sweet little China man?
Your name I want to know
With your lovely face so pale and wan
With a high diddle diddledy do!

Your high cheek bones – your screwed up mouth,
How beautiful they be!
And your eyes that ogle from north to south,
With a high diddle diddledy dee!

'Good folks' (and he shook his noddle ding-dong)
'It's enough for you to know,
That in spite of my eyebrows – two feet long,
I'm Miss Eliza's beau!'

Lear's earliest surviving piece of nonsense written in 1828.

CATCHING HIS EYES

He threw both of his eyes up to Heaven –
When another gentleman caught them instantly!

(Lear heard this amusing expression when he was a child and it was another factor in the development of his love of nonsense. He interpreted the words in this sketch made in 1846.)

WHEN MY OPES VOS BRIGHT

I slept: and back to my early days,
Did my wandering fancy roam,
When my heart was light
And my Opes vos bright
And my ome a appy one.

When I dreamed as I wàs young and hinnocent
And my art vos free from care,
And my parents smiled on their darling child,
And breathed for his life a prayer.

Once again I was rising before the sun,
For in childhood I was told,
If its early rays
On your head should play
It would turn each tress to gold.

Once again I was roaming through fields and flowers,
And I felt at each step new joys,
But I woke with a sigh that memory
Should revive what time destroys.

1836.

ADVICE TO YOUTH

It is a virtue in ingenious youth,
To leave off lying and return to truth,
For well it's known that all religious morals
Are caused by Bass's Ale and South Atlantic Corals!

September 1884.

THE YOUTHFUL COVE

Once on a time a youthful cove
As was a cheery lad
Lived in a villa by the sea,
The cove was not so bad.

The dogs and cats, the cows and ass,
The birds in cage or grove
The rabbits, hens, ducks, pony, pigs
All loved that cheery lad.

Seven folks – one female and six male –
Seized on that youthful cove;
They said, 'To edjukate this chap
Us seven it doth behove.'

The first his parrient was – who taught
The cove to read and ride,
Latin and Grammarithemetic,
And lots of things beside.

Says Pa, 'I'll spare no pains or time
Your school hours so to cut,
And square and fit, that you will make
No end of progress – *but* – .'

Says Mrs. Grey, 'I'll teach him French,
Pour parler dans cette pays –
Je cris, qu'll parlera bien,
Même comme un Francais – *Mais* –.'

Says Signor Gambinossi, 'Si,
Progresso si farà,
Lo voglio insegnare qui,
La lingua mai – *ma* –.'

Says Mr. Grump, 'Geology,
And Mathematics stiff
I'll teach the cove, who's sure to go
Ahead like blazes – *if* –.'

Says James, 'I'll teach him everyday
My Nastics: now and then
To stand upon his 'ed; and make
His mussels harder – *when* –.'

Says Signor Blanchi, 'Lascia far,
La musica da me,
Ben insegnata qui serà
Farà progresso – *Se* –.'

Says Edmund Lear, 'I'll make him draw
A Palace, or a hut,
Trees, mountains, rivers, cities, plains,
And p'rapps to paint them – *but* –.'

So all these seven joined hands and sang
This chorus by the sea:
'O! Ven his edjukation's done,
By! Vot a cove he'll *be*!'

                                        1856.

HOW TO REFUSE AN INVITATION TO DINNER

O Digby, my dear
It is perfectly clear
    That my mind will be horribly vext
If you happen to write
By ill luck to invite
    Me to dinner on Saturday next.

For this I should sigh at
That Mr. J. Wyatt
   Already has booked me, o dear!
So I could not send answer
To you – 'I'm your man, Sir!'
   Your loving fat friend, Edward Lear.
                    November 1863.

THE ILL-FITTING SHOE

O dear! how disgusting is life!
To improve it O what can we do?
Most disgusting is hustle and strife,
And of all things an ill-fitting shoe
An ill-fitting shoe
O bother an ill-fitting shoe!
                    January 1879.

THE BOWL OF PEACE

Washing my rosecoloured flesh and brushing my beard with
               a hairbrush,
Breakfast of tea, bread and butter, at nine o'clock in the
               morning,
Sending my carpet-bag onwards, I reach Twickenham
               Station,
Just as the big, buzzing, brown, booming, bottlegreen,
               bumblebizz boiler,
Stood on the point of departing for Richmond and
               England's metropolis.

I say (and if ever I said anything to the contrary I hearby
               retract it),

The Bowl of Peace.

I say – I took away altogether unconsciously your borrowed
                   white fillagree handkerchief;
After the lapse of a week I will surely return it,
And then you may either devour it, or keep it, or burn it –
Just as *you* please!

July 1859.

MRS. JAYPHER

Mrs. Jaypher found a wafer
Which she stuck upon a note;
This she took and gave the cook.
Then she went and bought a boat
Which she paddled down the stream
Shouting: 'Ice produces cream,
Beer when churned produces butter!
Henceforth all the words I utter
Distant ages thus shall note
From the Jaypher Wisdom-Boat!'

★ ★ ★

Mrs. Jaypher said it's safer
If you've lemons in your head
First to eat a pound of meat
And then to go at once to bed!

1885.

THE POBBLE WHO HAS NO TOES

(Complete Version)

I

The Pobble who has no toes
Had once as many as we;
When they said, 'Some day you may lose them all'
—
He replied, 'Fish fiddle de-dee!'
And his Aunt Jobiska made him drink,
Lavender water tinged with pink,
For she said, 'The World in general knows
There's nothing so good for a Pobble's toes!'

II

The Pobble who has no toes,
Swam across the Bristol Channel;
But before he set out he wrapped his nose,
In a piece of scarlet flannel.
For his Aunt Jobiska said, 'No harm
Can come to his toes if his nose is warm;
And it's perfectly known that a Pobble's toes
Are safe – provided he minds his nose.'

III

The Pobble swam fast and well
And when boats or ships came near him
He tinkledy-blinkledy-winkled a bell
So that all the world could hear him.
And all the Sailors and Admirals cried,
When they saw him nearing the farther side –
'He has gone to fish, for his Aunt Jobiska's
Runcible Cat with crimson whiskers!'

IV

The Pobble went gaily on,
To a rock by the edge of the water,
And there, a-eating of crumbs and cream,
Sat King Jampoodle's daughter.
Her cap was a root of beetroot red
With a hole cut out to insert her head;
Her gloves were yellow; her shoes were pink;
Her frock was green; and her name was Bink.

V

Said the Pobble, 'O, Princess Bink,
A-eating of crumbs and cream!
Your beautiful face has filled my heart
With the most profound esteem!
And when my Aunt Jobiska says, Man's life
Ain't worth a penny without a wife,
Whereby it will give me the greatest pleasure
If you'll marry me now, or when you've leisure'

VI

Said the Princess Blink, 'Oh, Yes!
I will certainly cross the Channel
And marry you then if you'll give me now
That lovely scarlet flannel!
And besides that flannel about your nose
I trust you will give me all your toes,
To place in my Pa's Museum collection,
As proofs of your deep genteel affection!'

VII

The Pobble unwrapped his nose,
And gave her the flannel so red,
Which, throwing her beetroot cap away,
She wreathed around her head.
And, one by one, he unscrewed his toes,
Which were made of the beautiful wood that grows
In his Aunt Jobiska's roorial park,
When the days are short and the nights are dark.

VIII

Said the Princes, 'O Pobble! my Pobble!
I'm yours for ever and ever!
I never will leave you my Pobble! my Pobble!
Never, and never, and never!'
Said the Pobble, 'My Binky! O bless your heart!'
But say – would you like at once to start
Without taking leave of your dumpetty Father
Jampoodle the King?' Said the Princess, 'Rather!'

IX

They crossed the Channel at once
And when boats and ships came near them,
They winkelty-binkelty-tinkled their bell
So that all the world could hear them.
And all the Sailors and Admirals cried
When they saw them swim to the farther side,
'There are no more fish for his Aunt Jobiska's
Runcible cat with crimson whiskers!'

X

They danced about all day,
All over the hills and dales;
They danced in every village town
In the North and the South of Wales.
And their Aunt Jobiska made them a dish
Of Mice and Buttercups fried with fish,
For she said, 'The World in general knows
Pobbles are happier without their toes!'

1884.

(*Editor's Note:* The published version of this poem in *Laughable Lyrics* has six verses, but Lear had originally written a total of ten: the fourth, fifth and six verses in the book replacing the last seven republished again here.)

SPOTS OF GREECE

Papa once went to Greece,
   And there I understand
He saw no end of lovely spots
   About that lovely land.

He talks about these spots of Greece
   To both Mama and me
Yet spots of Greece upon my dress
   They can't abear to see!

I cannot make it out at all –
   If ever on my Frock
They see the smallest Spot of Greece
   It gives them quite a shock!

Henceforth, therefore, to please them both
   These spots of Greece no more
Shall be upon my frock at all –
   Nor on my Pinafore!

1849.

A ROMAN MUSE

Says I to myself
Glad I shall be
When I am free
O Rome, from thee
And over the sea
High diddlydee!

Via Condotti, Rome, 6 January 1860.

A COACH RIDE

If you wish to see roads in perfection,
A climax of cart ruts and stones;
Or if you have the least predilection,
For breaking your neck or your bones;
If descents and ascents are inviting,
If your ankles are strangers to sprains,
If you'd cure a penchant for sliding,
Then to Peppering go by all means.

Take a coach some dark night in November,
A party of four within side;
Ah! I once had that jaunt I remember,
And really I pretty near died.
First across to my neighbour I tumbled,
Then into the next lady's lap,
For at every fresh rut we were jumbled,
And jolted at every new gap.

So that when we had finished our journey,
The coachman, who opened the door,
Found us tangled so very top turvey,
We rolled out in one bundle, all four.

And then we were so wisped together,
Legs, dresses, caps, arms blacks and whites
That some minutes lapsed before ever,
They got us completely to rights!

1829.

DINGLE BANK

He lived at Dingle Bank – he did;
　　He lived at Dingle Bank;
And in his garden was one Quail,
　　Four tulips, and a Tank:
And from his window he could see
The otion and the River Dee.

His house stood on a Cliff – it did;
　　Its aspic it was cool;
And many thousand little boys
　　Resorted to his school,
Where if of progress they could boast
He gave them heaps of buttered toast.

But he grew rabid-wroth – he did;
　　If they neglected books,
And dragged them to adjacent cliffs
　　With beastly Button Hooks,
And there with fatuous glee he threw
Them down into the otion blue.

And in the sea they swam – they did;
　　All playfully about,
And some eventually became
　　Sponges, or speckled trout;
But Liverpool doth all bewail
Their Fate – likewise his Garden Quail!

1850.

HOTEL GUESTS

The Octopeds and Reptiles,
They dine at 6 o'clock,
And having dined rush wildly out
Like an electric shock.

They hang about the bannisters
The corridors they block
And gabbling, bothering
A most unpleasant flock.

They hang about the bannisters
Upon the stairs they flock
And howly-gabbling all the while
The corridors they block!

Summer, 1882.

THE BOOK LEFT OUT

When leaving this beautiful, blessed Brianza,
My trunks were all corded and locked except one;
But that was unfilled, through a dismal Mancanza,
Nor could I determine on what should be done.

For out of three volumes (all equally bulky),
Which – travelling, I constantly carry about –

There was room for but two – so though angry and sulky,
I had to decide as to which to leave out.

A Bible! A Shakespeare! A Tennyson! – stuffing
And stamping and squeezing were wholly in vain!
A Tennyson! A Shakespeare! A Bible! – All puffing
Was useless, and one of the three must remain.

And this was the end – and it's truth and no libel,
A-weary with thinking I settled my doubt,
As I packed and sent off both the Shakespeare and Bible,
And finally left only Tennyson out!

Summer 1885.

THE FLY AND THE PAINTER

But, ah! (the Landscape painter said),
A brutal fly walks on my head
And my bald skin doth tickle;
And so I stop distracted quite,
(With itching skin for who can write?)
In a most disgusting pickle!

November 1861.

THE CUMMERBUND

I

She sat upon her Dobie,
To watch the Evening Star,
And all the Punkahs as they passed,
Cried, 'My! how fair you are!'
Around her bower, with quivering leaves,
The tall Kamsamahs grew,

And kitmutgars in wild festoons
Hung down from Tchokis blue.

II

Below her home the river rolled,
With soft meloobious sound,
Where golden-finned Chuprassies swam,
In myriads circling round.
Above, on tallest trees remote,
Green Ayahs perched alone,
And all night long the Mussak moan'd
Its melancholy tone.

III

And where the purple Nullahs threw,
Their branches far and wide,
And silvery Goreewallahs flew,
In silence, side by side,
The little Bheestie's twittering cry,
Rose on the flagrant air,
And oft the angry Jampan howled
Deep in his hateful lair.

IV

She sat upon her Dobie,
She heard the Nimmak hum,
When all at once a cry arose,
'The Cummerbund is come!'
In vain she fled – with open jaws,
The angry monster followed,
And so (before assistance came),
That Lady Fair was swallowed!

V

They sought in vain for every bone,
Respectfully to bury,
They said, 'Hers was a dreadful fate!'
(And Echo answered, 'Very!')
They nailed her Dobie to the wall,

Where last her form was seen,
And underneath they wrote these words,
In yellow, blue and green:–

'Beware, ye Fair! Ye Fair, beware!
Nor sit out late at night,
Lest horrid Cummerbunds should come,
And swallow you outright!

July 1874.

THE SIX CHICKEY BIRDS

Mrs. Blue Dickey-bird went out a-walking with her six
            Chickey Birds.
She carried a parasol and wore a bonnet of green silk.
The first little Chickey Bird had daises growing out of his
            head and wore boots because of
            the dirt.
The second little Chickey Bird wore a hat, for fear it would
            rain.
The third little Chickey Bird carried a jug of water.
The fourth little Chickey Bird carried a muff, to keep her
            wings warm.
The fifth little Chickey Bird was round as a ball.
And the sixth little Chickey Bird walked on his head, to
            save his feet.

1837.

A Bed-Time Verse

The Chough and the Crow to roost are
gone,
The owl sits on the tree,
Both child and nurse are fast-asleep,
And closed is every flower.

1842.

Epitaph

Beneath these high Cathedral stairs,
Lies the remains of Susan Pares.
Here name was Wiggs, it was not Pares,
But Pares was put to rhyme with stairs.

1838.

Nonsense Verses

In the hundred years since Edward Lear's death a number of
further nonsense verses have been unearthed by scholars and
published in either anthologies or limited editions of a few
hundred copies. It has, however, proved impossible to bring
together all these verses in this book, so instead I have conten-
ted myself with a selection of twenty-four of the most interesting and unusual items – none of which are included in the

popular editions of Lear's works. A few notes by way of explanation are called for.

The first item concerning 'the Old Man with a Book' features Lear himself and was addressed to Chichester Fortescue, exhorting him to buy one of his collections. (Another later item, the 'Old Man who felt Pert' in his rose-coloured shirt, depicts Lear, too!) The second verse about 'a Sick Man of Tobago' is not actually *by* Lear, but appeared in a book entitled *The Anecdotes & Adventures of Fifteen Gentlemen* published in 1822. These lines were shown to Lear by a 'valued friend' and – as he subsequently admitted – they so captured his imagination as a format for giving expression to the nonsense which bubbled inside him, that they proved the inspiration for all the work which was to make him famous. The limerick appears here complete with Lear's own impression of the unhappy man from Tobago, which he drew in 1840.

The 'Old Sailor of Compton' and 'an Old Man of New York' actually appeared in the now extremely rare first edition of *A Book of Nonsense* published in 1846, but were inexplicably deleted from the second and have not been republished since. The 'Young Person of Chertsey' is a real curiosity, too, for it was the first draft of a now very familiar limerick. As enthusiasts of Lear's work will know, the person of Chertsey who sank underground was actually an old lady! We can only speculate on *why* the author felt such vigorous exercise more likely to be undertaken by a veteran.

The final sequence of three limericks featuring the old man, small child and puppy from Narkunda were inspired during Lear's trip through India in April 1874 when he passed through the town of that name on the way to Simla. They are the only verses to share a common location.

There was an Old Man with a Book,
Who said, 'Only look! Only look!
Obsquation – obsgration – at Waterloo Station,
Enquire if there ain't such a book!'

★

There was a Sick Man of Tobago
Lived long on Rice-Gruel and Sago.
Till one day, to his bliss, the physician said this,
'To a roast leg of mutton you may go!'

★

There was an Old Sailor of Compton,
Whose vessel a rock it once bump'd on,
The shock was so great, that it damaged the pate,
Of that singular sailor of Compton!

★

There was an Old Man of New York,
Who murdered himself with a fork,
But nobody cried, though he very soon died,
For that silly old man of New York!

★

There was an Old Man of Carlisle,
Who was left on a desolate isle,
Where he fed upon cakes, and lived wholly with snakes,
Who danced with that man of Carlisle!

★

There was a Young Person of Chertsey,
Who made a remarkable curtsey
She turned round and round, till she sank underground,
Which bewildered the people of Chertsey!

★

There was an Old Person of Cheam,
Who said, 'It is just like a dream,
When I play on the drum, and wear rings on my thumb,
In the beautiful meadows of Cheam!'

There was an Old Man of Bombay,
Sat a smoking one very hot day,
When a bird (called a snipe), flew away with his pipe,
Which grieved this Old Man of Bombay!

*

There was an Old Man of Orleans
Who was given to eating of beans,
Till once out of sport, he swallowed a quart,
That dyspeptic Old Man of Orleans!

*

There was an Old Man who felt pert,
When he wore a pale rose-coloured shirt.
When they said, 'Is it pleasant?' He cried, 'Not at present,
It's a *leetle* too short is my shirt!'

*

There was an Old Person of Twickenham,
Who whipped his four horses to quicken 'em,
When they stood on one leg, he said faintly, I beg
We may go back directly to Twickenham!'

*

There was an Old Man of the Dee,
Who always was partial to tea,
Buttered toast he abhorred, and by Muffins was bored,
That uncommon Old Man of the Dee!

★

There was an Old Person of Harrow,
Who bought a mahogany barrow,
For he said to his wife, 'You're the joy of my life,
And I'll wheel you all day in this barrow!'

★

There was an Old Soldier of Bicester,
Who was walking one day with his sister,
When a bull with one poke, tossed her into an oak,
Before that old gentleman missed her!

★

There was an Old Woman of Leith
Who had the most dolorous teeth,
So she had a new set. 'I'll eat quantities yet,'
Said that fortunate Woman of Leith!

★

There was an Old Person of Brussels,
Who lived on Brandy and Mussels,
When he rushed through the town, he knocked most people
down,
Which distressed all the people of Brussels!

★

There was an Old Man who forgot,
That his tea was excessively hot,
When they said, 'Let it cool,' he answered, 'You fool!
I shall pour it back in the pot!'

★

There was an Old Person of Diss,
Who said, 'It is this! It is this!'
When they said, 'What? Or which?', he jumped into a ditch,
Which absorbed that Old Person of Diss!

★

There was a Old Person of Paxo
Who complained when the fleas bit his back so,
But they gave him a chair, and impelled him to swear,
Which relieved that Old Person of Paxo.

★

There was an Old Person of Bradley,
Who sang all so loudly and sadly,
With a poker and tongs, he beat time to his songs,
That melodious Old Person of Bradley!

★

There was an Old Man of the Hills,
Who lived upon Syrup of Squills,
Which he drank all night long, to the sound of a gong,
That persistent Old Man of the Hills!

★

There was an Old Man of Narkunda,
Whose voice was like peals of loud thunder,
It shivered the hills, into Colveynth pills,
And destroyed half the trees of Narkunda!

★

There was a Small Child of Narkunda,
Who said, 'Don't you hear, that is Thunder!'
But they said, 'It's the Bonzes' amazing responses
In a temple eight miles from Narkunda!'

★

There lived a Small Puppy at Narkunda,
Who sought for the best tree to bark under,
Which he found, and then said, 'Now I can call out Bow
Wow,
Underneath the best cedar in Narkunda!'

EIGHT

A
LEARNED
QUIZ

(From *The Spectator*, 17 September 1887)

A friend of this journal who is deeply versed in Mr. Edward Lear's Nonsense books has drawn up this list of questions for the amusement of our readers.

1. What do you gather from a study of Mr. Lear's works to have been the prevalent characteristics of the inhabitants of Gretna, Prague, Thermopylae, Wick and Hong Kong?

2. State briefly what historical events are connected with Ischia, Chertsey, Whitehaven, Boulak and Jellibolee.

3. Comment, with illustrations, upon Mr. Lear's use of the following words: Runcible, propitious, dolomphious, borascible, fizzgiggious, himmeltanious, tumble-dum-down, sponge-taneous.

4. Enumerate accurately all the animals who lived on the Quangle Wangle's Hat – and explain how the Quangle Wangle was enabled at once to enlighten his five travelling companions as to the true nature of the Co-operative Cauliflower.

5. What were the names of the five daughters of the Old Person of China, and what was the purpose for which the Old Man of the Dargle purchased six barrels of Gargle?

6. Collect notices of King Xerxes in Mr. Lear's works, and state your theory – if you have any – as to the character and appearance of Nupiter Piffkin.

7. Draw pictures of the Plum-pudding Flea and the Moppsikon Floppsikon Bear, and state by whom waterproof tubs were first used.

8. 'There was an Old Man at a station – Who made a promiscuous oration.' What bearing may we assume the foregoing couplet to have upon Mr. Lear's political views?